Dear Evelyn & Lou,

I think you will know some of the people in this book!

All my love,

Seima (Shula)

Taking Care of Mom, Taking Care of Me

Coping with a Relative's Illness & Death

Sima Devorah Schloss

The Judaica Press, Inc.

Library of Congress Cataloging-in-Publication Data

Schloss, Sima Devorah, 1955-
   Taking care of mom, taking care of me : coping with a
relative's illness and death / by Sima Devorah Schloss.
       p. cm.
   ISBN 1-880582-97-X (hardcover)
   1. Aging parents--Care. 2. Adult children of aging parents. 3.
Sandwich generation. I. Title.
   HQ1063.6 .S354 2002
   306.874'0846--dc21

                                          2002014371

THE JUDAICA PRESS, INC.
123 Ditmas Avenue
Brooklyn, New York 11218
718-972-6200   800-972-6201
info@judaicapress.com
www.judaicapress.com

Manufactured in the United States of America

DEDICATED TO THE MEMORIES OF

❧

My parents, Melvin & Selma Kesselman, o.b.m.

My in-laws, Harry & Lillian Schloss, o.b.m.

My aunts, Shirley Strum and Annette Stiglitz, o.b.m.

My grandparents (Mom and Pop),
Adolf & Ruth Kesselman, o.b.m.

MAY THEIR SOULS BENEFIT FROM THE MERIT OF THIS BOOK.

TABLE of CONTENTS

ACKNOWLEDGEMENTS

With appreciation for my partners in taking care of others, my husband Robert Schloss, and my daughter Ilana Schloss. Thanks also to our friends, Lori Schroeder and Karen Hedges, for their help and support and to Innocile and Lorraine, two very dedicated aides.

Thank you to the staff at the Hebrew Home for the Aged for taking such loving care of my grandmother.

Special thanks to Rabbi Dr. Abraham J. Twerski for writing the foreword even before anyone would agree to publish this book. Thanks also to Dr. Blema Feinstein for all her teachings, to Rachel Witty for once more helping with the preliminary editing, to Dipti Shah from Staples for her tireless photocopying and to Shirley Lamm for her encouragement.

Special thanks to Nachum Shapiro, Aryeh Mezei and the Judaica Press staff for taking another chance on me. Thanks also to Bonnie Goldman for the beautiful book design, Rena Joseph for expert editing and Zisi Berkowitz for her painstaking formatting.

With deep gratitude to the *Ribono Shel Olam* for helping me with every step of this project.

FOREWORD

V irtually nothing else in Judaism is given the importance of *gemilas chasodim*, acts of loving-kindness. The patriarch Abraham, father of our nation, is praised most for his *gemilas chasodim*. The Talmud emphasizes its importance when it states that the Torah begins and ends with acts of kindness.

Add to this the emphasis the Torah attributes to honoring one's parents. "Honoring one's parents is equivalent to honoring Me," God says. Nothing, therefore, could be of greater merit than loving-kindness toward one's parents.

In recent times we have come into circumstances that require special attention. Thanks to some marvelous medical advances, the average life span has significantly increased. More people than ever before are living into their eighties and nineties. However, medicine has not yet found a solution for some of the conditions that occur in later life. Elderly people may be limited in their function by chronic respiratory disease and arthritis. They may not be able to care adequately for themselves. Alzheimers disease is particularly disabling.

Younger people, who are raising their own children, often find it necessary to help care for their parents. The term "sandwich generation" describes people who find themselves needing to provide for both their parents and their children. There may not be enough energy to go around. Trying to do everything for everyone may so drain a person's energy that one becomes exhausted, and, ironically, may then not be able to do anything for anyone.

It is possible, though, to distribute one's time and energy so that what needs to be done is done, while maintaining one's health. Such calculations require sound, logical and realistic planning. But these are circumstances that are profoundly affected by emotion, which can preclude logical thinking.

When flying in a plane, the flight attendant announces, "In case of a drop in cabin pressure, oxygen masks will appear." She then gives instruction on their use, and adds, "If you are traveling with a child, put your own mask on first and then tend to the child." This is not about being selfish. If you try to put the child's mask on while you are deprived of oxygen, you may be so confused that you put it over his ear rather than his nose. The moral: You must take care of yourself in order to be able to help others.

Sima Schloss shares her personal experiences to shed light on these delicate issues. Her fascinating journey offers comfort and advice for those who find themselves in the role of caregivers.

—Rabbi Abraham J. Twerski, M.D.

CHAPTER ONE

TAKING CARE
of MOM

S ometimes the details and timing of circumstances that emerge in life can exert an enormous impact on how we think and feel. Then we have a choice. We can ignore the events and continue our lives as usual, or we can view them as opportunities for growth and change.

As we hear news of more Israeli victims of terrorism each day, we Jews are challenged to search our souls and contemplate the purpose of our very existence. When the World Trade Center buildings were destroyed, along with thousands of people, the population of the United States, and perhaps the entire world, experienced exactly this type of circumstance, an event of enormous impact. Collectively, we all face choices. How will this event affect us? Will we change our lives, and in what way?

In the space of five years, I experienced the sickness and loss of seven close family members. Most of the other older members of my family passed away. My grandmother was experiencing incapacitating dementia. I had to make these choices on a personal level. Would I just keep going? Would I use these sad moments as a catalyst for change?

Mom, as we affectionately called my grandmother, moved in with us at the end of November 1997. It had become too hard for her to live alone. For most of her adult life, she had lived in the Bronx. Then she lived for almost twenty years in an apartment for senior citizens in Manhattan. In the last year, she had become forgetful. She had some health care help but the management of her building did not think she was safe. They wanted her to have more help. But she refused. "After all," she would say, "I need time to rest." Mom felt she would not get any rest if there were strangers around.

Then came the pressure. They threatened that she would have to move to a nursing home if she did not accept more assistance. For years I had encouraged her to move in with me. She had refused each invitation.

She had lived on her own for over thirty years, since my grandfather had died. But in her confusion, she became frightened. She heard voices and thought that people were breaking into her apartment to steal her things. She would lose her keys and become house bound until I was able to bring over another set. So I tried again.

"Maybe it's time to move in with us, Mom," I implored, again.

"Maybe you're right," she finally acquiesced.

My Aunt Annette had lung cancer. So I was rushing to help Mom make the move before her daughter passed away. How can a person bear the loss of a child while living alone? Little did I know that it would be my father who would die first.

My father was hospitalized. I juggled the responsibilities for my grandmother and father for a little over a month. And then he was gone. Mom and I were sitting *shiva*. It had been raining since the funeral on Tuesday. Sometimes a downpour. Sometimes just a mist. The sun came out just as we were setting up the Shabbat candles (the candles that Jews light just before sunset on Friday to mark the beginning of Shabbat). We were observing the week of *shiva*, the seven-day period of mourning. Some authorities rule that the mourner should not leave the house during this week except on Shabbat to go to services at the synagogue, but it never occurred to me to inquire about going out. We had been in since Tuesday, and I thought that it would be good for my grandmother to stretch her legs with a short walk. We lit the candles and I turned to her and said, "The sun is finally out. Maybe you would like to take a walk with me before it gets dark?"

"Okay," was all she replied.

We put on our coats and started slowly down the street. Mom was ninety years old on that particular day, so walking was fairly slow. She used to be the best walker in the family. There was a time when she could out-walk any of us. But that was many years ago.

As we walked, we talked about the week.

She began, "No one knows how I am suffering. You know it was my son that I lost," she explained, as if I didn't know.

"I know, Mom. He was my father," I reminded her gently.

"That's right. He was. It's very hard to lose a son. He was my firstborn. And my daughter is also very sick."

"Yes, Mom. Nobody can imagine how hard it is for you."

"You know, all of those people came and they kept talking and telling jokes, like I wasn't even there, and all the time my heart was breaking."

"They meant well, Mom. It's just that many people don't know what to say at a time like this, so they just keep talking to fill up the silence."

"They don't know my pain."

"No, they don't."

"I buried my firstborn son this week."

"Yes, Mom. I know."

My father had died only three days earlier. This was the first time that Mom had focused her thoughts on the fact that her son had passed away. Sometimes she said it was her husband or her father that was gone. She seemed to slip in and out of the reality that was upon us. But, on that walk, it all came together.

She was right. The week of *shiva* had been an ordeal. People coming and going. Nobody knowing what to say. Idle conversation about nonsense that I had no patience for. Now I understand why the rabbis say that when you visit a house of mourning, you should just go and sit quietly. Let the mourner speak first, or just sit in silence. Most of our visitors didn't know about that.

The *shiva* period wasn't all awful. There were heartwarming stories and conversations about my father, and there were kind gestures of food and help. I work as a recreation therapist at the Long Island State Veterans Home. When the recreation staff paid a condolence call, they brought their warmth and understanding along with them. Of course, we work with old and dying people every day, so dealing with death and speaking words of comfort are a normal part of our day.

Thank God for Shabbat, a brief respite when public mourning is not allowed. Afterwards, there would be two more days left and the *shiva* week would be over. And then what? Time to heal? Judaism designates a whole year of mourning for parents. I had come to understand the wisdom of this law.

Our family had become all too familiar with death in recent years. First it was my Aunt Shirley followed by my mother Selma. Then three years later, my husband's mother Lillian. Two years later, my husband's father Harry died, followed by my father five months after that. At some point I would have to come to terms with death, wrestle with the ideas about what happens to the human soul after the physical body dies. But not yet, not now. At this point, I was just getting through each day.

My grandmother brought me back from my thoughts.

"Look how nice it is out now," Mom exclaimed.

"Yes," I answered. "It's hard to believe it is the middle of January."

❧   ❧   ❧

Is it a blessing to live to ninety? Everyone was gone — her husband, her sisters, her brothers, her friends and now her son. Mom sat *shiva* for eleven people. Who would sit for her?

But I believe that life is a gift and we must do the

best we can with whatever God gives us, until such time as He sees fit. I used to argue this point with my father. He believed in assisted suicide, in death with dignity. In accordance with Jewish law, I believe that life and death should be determined by God alone.

My father is gone. I guess that I won that argument, even if only by default. The more pressing matter was trying to determine the best course of action for Mom.

But I am getting ahead of myself. Mom was the last in a line of aging relatives for whose life and health I had taken responsibility. I am a recovering codependent, somewhat addicted to taking care of other people. Now this might not sound like such a bad thing. As a Jew, it even seemed like the right thing to do. The problem was that my taking care of others arose out of a sense of both responsibility and control. The job became so consuming that I no longer had any time or energy to take care of myself, and it also robbed others of their ability to care for themselves. This state was intensified when my father was living with me. I had assumed that it was my responsibility to schedule his doctor appointments, prepare all of his meals and wash his laundry. It never occurred to me to hire help or send some laundry out when I felt too overwhelmed. Earlier, when my mother had passed away, I had felt guilty, as if I could have somehow found a cure for her cancer if I had only searched harder!

As a Jew, I know that I am commanded to perform acts of loving-kindness, including visiting the sick. I tried my best to be attentive to my loved ones as they endured sickness and faced death. In the beginning of the five years, I tried so hard that I lost myself in the process. I was so addicted to taking care of other people, I forgot to take care of myself.

Then I found Codependents Anonymous (CoDA), a self-help organization that uses meetings and the twelve steps of recovery to build healthier lives. I used the steps to forge a healthy balance between kindness to others and kindness to myself. Going to meetings and drawing on inspiration from other people's stories enabled me to use the events of my life as avenues for improving myself both physically and spiritually. By the time my grandmother came to live with my family, I was able to find the healthy balance that I needed to care for her and cope with my father's illness.

I used to think that I was the expert on the subject of loss and grief. Then I attended a meeting on that topic at a retreat with JACS (Jewish Alcoholics, Chemically dependent persons and Significant others). Listening to people's stories about their terrible losses was a humbling experience. I did not lose a spouse or a child or any young family member. I was not estranged from my parents and unable to be a part of their lives, connect with them or make closure. Although I considered the losses to be too soon without much time between losses, I must admit that they were in the realm of the natural flow of life. An older generation passing while the younger generation continues to live.

I no longer consider myself an expert, but my experience gave me insight and strength that I would like to share with you. I will tell you about three people — my father Melvin, my father-in-law Harry, and my grandmother Ruth, whom I still call Mom. Each in turn came to live in our home. Each of these dear people had an impact on my family, on our relationship with each other and on my overall attitude toward life. I will also tell you about my beloved mother and two close aunts. Living with and caring for older people can be difficult and often heartbreaking, but this experience also creates a possibility of attaining both wisdom and joy.

CHAPTER TWO

TO LOVE
and TO LOSE

I can't really talk about my father without including my mother. Their lives were intertwined, and their marriage was one of loyalty and devotion.

They met when they were sixteen. When I was sorting through their possessions to get ready for the sale of their home, I made an unexpected discovery of letters that were written by my father to my mother during their courtship. The focus of his life completely changed when he met my mother. She became his world. He would often say, "I do not know why your mother married me. What could she possibly have seen in me? She could have done much better."

If there was ever a disagreement, no matter who was right, my father would apologize and defer to my mother. I realized that there were big things discussed out of the hearing range of us children, where he did not follow her suggestions. All the same, in front of us he used to say, "Selma makes all of the small decisions and I save all of the big decisions to make myself. Of course, in forty years of marriage, there hasn't been a big decision yet."

It seemed to me that they did almost everything together with the exception of his pinochle games and her mah-jongg parties. They went to concerts, to the opera and bowling. They played bridge, went out for dinner and loved to go to shows. All of the vacations were family vacations, often with extended family members such as aunts, uncles, cousins and, of course, Mom.

Mom went with us to Washington. Mom, Aunt Annette and my sister Valerie, newly married, with her husband Gerry, went with us to Florida. That was when we all crossed the street in a single file walking like Charlie Chaplin.

Aunt Shirley and my cousin Vicki came with us when we went to Quebec. We were watching all of the children in the pool. We laughed so hard when Aunt Shirley said, "Isn't it wonderful how all of these children can speak French!"

When I was little, my mother and I used to spend time at the beach in the summer, along with my sister Valerie, my Aunt Shirley and my cousin Vicki. Aunt Shirley used to make us boats out of the sand and put in wooden sticks for the controls. We would play for hours.

I was in my late thirties when my secure world began to unravel. First, Aunt Shirley was diagnosed with acute leukemia. Life began to fall into a pattern of hospital visits. The hospital quickly turned my aunt into a non-person. I remember once when they took her for a test she told us that they left her in a cold hallway waiting for hours. Chemo, blood tests, IV's stuck into her arm. And there she was, this entire time, still concerned about others, and worrying about how her roommate was doing. Six weeks later she was transferred to intensive care.

The day before she died, I was the first to arrive at the hospital. Aunt Shirley was on a respirator. Although she had signed a DNR (do not resuscitate) order, the nurse said that she had gone into a state of panic when she felt that she could not breathe and asked for help. She was afraid to die. They hooked her up to a respirator. I wondered, "Will I be afraid? Will I be able to remember that this life was meant to be temporary and that, although I will turn to dust, my soul will continue to exist? Will I find strength in the words of Maimonides, who described the eternal spiritual existence of the soul as 'a bliss beyond which there is nothing more blissful'? Will I remember all that I have learned about the soul and the afterlife, or will I also panic?"

And now what about my aunt who was already lying so frail before me? It was obvious that she was dying, and yet some doctor wanted to do still another procedure on her to more accurately monitor her medication. I stopped him. I said, "You will wait until her children arrive!" The family agreed, "No more guinea pig procedures." Only medication that would alleviate her pain. I didn't know it at the time but we had a basis in Jewish law. A person in their last stages of death should be kept comfortable but only minimally touched, as we are only required to prolong life but not the process of dying.

But I did not know all this at the time. I asked myself instead, "Was she still there somewhere in that cold and almost lifeless body?" Her fear was gone. Did she know that she was headed for a better place?

That night the phone rang. I heard my mother's voice. "Sit down. I have something to tell you." I figured that my aunt had passed away. I tried to clear my head. "I got the test results," my mother said. "I have endometrial cancer." There was that big "C" word, again. My mother had cancer. This meant more hospitals, more chemo.

Aunt Shirley passed away the very next day.

A month later, my Aunt Annette was diagnosed with breast cancer.

I don't know if I ever came to terms with the fact that the matriarchs of my family were all afflicted with cancer. Sometimes I still think, "So what if they are all together now in a better place. What about me? I still need them. It isn't fair!"

I try to imagine them all in a wonderful place. The Torah promises us that there is another life after this one, more beautiful than can be imagined, but it directs us to maintain our focus and emphasis on our present existence. Our present existence, our earthly life, is often filled with struggling and suffering, but we are told that we must fight to continue on and to live each moment that God has given us to the fullest. In fact, those very difficulties are what give us an opportunity to develop our spiritual greatness.

The difficult times don't always appear to be so beneficial. When my mother was diagnosed with endometrial cancer in September of 1990, I certainly couldn't see anything good. First came the operation, and later, the chemo treatments. My father's life began to fall apart. He was the constant fixture at my mother's side whenever she was hospitalized. My father, who is left handed, had already been suffering with tremors in his left hand from Parkinson's. Now he needed to learn how to write with his right hand. Still he kept working.

My mother's physical condition continued to deteriorate, and my father's mental state took a plunge.

I tried to help whenever I could. I sent my mother to a holistic doctor who did intravenous vitamin therapy. My mother went, but it was not for her. I searched the reports in the medical library hoping to find success stories of effective treatments for my mother's kind of cancer. I called a doctor in London who was having success with one particular treatment. My mother's own physician did not exactly appreciate my input and disregarded the therapies suggested by the holistic doctor. He forbade my mother to take any megavitamins. He said that they might interfere with her chemo. He didn't seem at all interested in the information that I sent him from the doctor in London. By the time another doctor decided to try the treatment of the English physician it was too late.

For all of my father's happiness with my mother, he struggled with depression for many years. Chemical? Emotional? I do not know. His psychiatrist said chemical, and prescribed medication. My father called him his drug pusher.

With my mother's cancer supposedly "cured" it became apparent that her illness had been too much for my father. He suffered a mental breakdown and was hospitalized. I was so angry with him. How could he do this to my mother? She needed all of her strength to recover from the cancer and instead she had to run now to the hospital to see him. The psychiatric unit had very limited hours, an hour in the afternoon and another hour and a half in the evening. Sometimes she traveled the thirty minutes to and from the hospital twice a day. Other times she just stayed in the area, waiting for the evening hours. I know that my father did not really choose to be sick anymore than my mother chose to have cancer, but I still blamed him for it. I felt that he should have somehow held himself together. My mother seemed so weak and vulnerable that I never considered that visiting my father was something that my mother chose to do.

Life seemed difficult now. I tried juggling my part-time job with the needs of my husband Bob, and the needs of his business. Then, there were also the many responsibilities of raising my six-year-old daughter Ilana. All of that, together with being there for my mother as much time as I could while also visiting my father, left me feeling that I was always on the run.

But there were also some wonderful moments when I would visit my mother and we would sit and talk. Sometimes I would go with her to visit my father in the hospital, keep her company and help with the driving. Once we got to the hospital too early for visiting hours, so we went down to the harbor nearby and watched the ducks and boats on the water. A few moments of peace and quiet.

No sooner than my father was discharged, after a two-month hospitalization, my mother's cancer resurfaced.

She fought the cancer. Exercise. Positive imagery tapes. Rest. She was so beautiful. You would never have known that she was dying of cancer from the way she looked, even on her last day.

All this time I had been praying, begging God each day for her to live. My father told me later that the doctor had told him that there was no hope. My father had prayed that she would be free of the terrible pain that afflicts many cancer patients. On the night before she died we knew that it was only a matter of time. The nurse was still putting those tight stockings on her that were supposed to prevent blood clots. They looked so uncomfortable. Finally I said to the nurse, "Maybe we shouldn't bother. Let's make her more comfortable." The nurse replied, "I guess you are right. I just can't believe that she's dying."

I will never forget that night. All the way home the same thought persisted in my mind: She is dying, I better turn around and go back. When I got home, I gathered some food and books and then went right back to the hospital to spend the night.

I sat all night and read from the Book of Psalms. By the morning I had recited the entire book. My mother talked all night to some unseen presence. The nurse and I stayed with her. We kept asking her, "Are you all right? Are you in any pain? Do you need any medication?" She would interrupt her conversation, which seemed to be taking place in another world, just long enough to answer no to our questions, and then she went right back to her private conversation. I think she was fighting to live right up until the end.

My father and sister arrived in the morning. Do I stay? Do I go home? I couldn't decide. I had brought a little food with me but now it was gone. Perhaps if I had asked, the hospital might have had some kosher food, but I never thought of asking. I was so hungry and tired at this point. I think I also craved the comfort of my husband and my daughter. I wanted to hold them close and to know that I still had family of my own. If I had comprehended that her death was imminent, if I had known that Jewish law admonishes those in the presence of a dying person not to leave, perhaps I would not have left. Perhaps, though, it was easier for her to let go with me gone.

Having returned home, I called my sister Valerie, who was at the hospital. She said that my mother's breathing was getting slower and slower, and put the phone on hold. I sat at the kitchen table with my husband and daughter. All of a sudden it started to pour. My sister came back on the phone. My mother was gone. My daughter Ilana said, "I think that God is cry-ing for Grandma." Perhaps He was crying for all of us.

My father and sister approved my request for a *shomer*, a watchman to guard my mother's body as required by Jewish law until the funeral. They also agreed to a *taharah*, the ritual washing of the body. My mother died on a Tuesday. Out of respect for the dead, a Jew is supposed to be buried quickly, within twenty-four hours. My father decided to wait an extra day because our rabbi was not available on Wednesday. The funeral would be called instead for Thursday.

That Wednesday was the longest day of my life. I couldn't eat, and I couldn't sleep. I sat outside in the backyard trying to think of what I could say at her memorial service. I sat so long that my legs got stiff. But I wrote a eulogy. I recalled what a wonderful mother and person she had been. Then I said, "I was so lucky to have her as my mother. There could never be a right time to lose my mother."

God gives us our loved ones for temporary safe-keeping, like a precious stone. Then, when He decides it is time, He takes them back. I would never have been ready to give up my mother. I will always feel her loss, but I will be eternally grateful for the time I had with her.

Thursday finally arrived. My sister's rabbi, who was officiating, gave each of the mourners a black rib-bon as a sign of mourning. My sister's family interpreted this liberally and included many members of the extended family in addition to the immediate mourners. One of the Orthodox rabbis present, who wanted to be sure that I was conforming to *halacha*, to Jewish law, rushed over to me to make sure that I was not wearing a black ribbon. He explained that wearing a black ribbon is not considered to be an acceptable substitute for actually rending one's garment. Was my shirt torn in the appropriate manner? The rabbi had nothing to fear. I had already been well advised!

Valerie and I had agreed with each other that nobody but members of the family and friends would be allowed to carry the casket out of respect for our mother.

Then there was the matter of covering the grave. Rabbi Daniel Goldstein, of blessed memory, who was not a young man at the time, demonstrated by his determined shoveling that, according to traditional practice, the grave should be filled in by the mourners and by family and friends, out of respect for the deceased. Although some authorities say that a partial covering is enough, we followed Rabbi Goldstein's example and completed the job ourselves.

After the special Burial *Kaddish* (the prayer for the departed) was recited, everyone began to leave. I felt too paralyzed to move. I had the feeling that my mother was somehow still present as long as I stood by her grave. I feared that the moment I left, she would be gone forever. Everyone got into their cars. I was left alone. I don't know how long I stood by her grave. Eventually I reluctantly returned to my parents' home to begin sitting *shiva*.

What did I find there? Was this a party? Why did this seem to me like some kind of family celebration? There seemed to be swarms of people, eating, drinking, talking. I stood there, not knowing what I should do. I was so tired and there was so much noise. Finally, I was saved by Rabbi Goldstein who had me sit down and who then told someone to bring me something to eat. I was brought food that my friends had provided. Jewish law states that food should be provided for the mourner because a mourner might not eat if left on their own, and a mourner is not permitted to fast. That was true for me. I wasn't very hungry. I didn't eat much again until a friend brought me homemade kosher sausage and spaghetti a few days later. The aroma was enticing. Finally, I regained my appetite.

Although my father no longer observed most Jewish rituals, he still wanted to say *Kaddish* three times a day for that week, as he had done for an entire year for his father many years before. My daughter Ilana, who was seven now, had been very close to my mother and was very saddened by her death. I felt that she really needed my support. Because Jewish law does not obligate a woman to say *Kaddish*, I decided not to attend the daily 6:00 a.m. morning *minyan* (prayer service), which took place at my father's house. As a woman, I was exempt from this obligation, and I was thankful for that, because it gave me time with Ilana before she went to school. Then I joined my father at his house for the rest of the day and was present for the afternoon and evening services. Our community's rabbi organized a *minyan* every day for each service, which was no small feat in our neighborhood made up of mostly non-committed Jews. We drew the *minyan* from various Long Island congregations. I could see how the *minyanim* gave strength to my father. They gave him a reason to get up and face each day.

My husband left at the crack of dawn to get fresh bread and cake for the morning worshippers. This was not so easy because the closest kosher bakery was more than fifteen miles away. But Bob felt that if people were coming to help out, especially for a mitzvah, the least we could do was serve them fresh food. I learned later that it was more appropriate for the visitors to bring the food and serve the mourners, not the other way around. At least it was my husband, who was not an immediate relative, taking care of things, and not me. Bob was a wonderful support throughout this sad time and the many more that would follow in the next six years. I came to realize that the hard times can make or break a marriage. Our difficult times drew us closer together. We became united in the mission of trying to take care of the older generation and then coping with our losses as they each, in turn, passed away.

The *shiva* for my mother was a time of unity for my whole family. My sister Valerie and Mom stayed for several days with my father. It was a wonderful time of closeness and reminiscing. After the crowds of that first day, we had a lot of time to just sit and talk to each other. I remember that once we were all gathered around the table laughing about something that had happened in the past when someone came to pay a *shiva* call. We were all embarrassed. They were coming to comfort us and found us all laughing.

I learned that, according to Jewish custom, people should not make *shiva* calls on the first three days. Rather, this time should be reserved for the immediate family as a private opportunity for facing the loss and dealing with the intense grief. We certainly did a lot of both crying and laughing in those first few days and found immense comfort in each other's presence.

When making a *shiva* call, it is customary to let the mourners take the lead in how much they want to talk and what they want to talk about. I talked about being so thankful for my wonderful family. My mother had lived for so many years in close proximity with my Aunt Shirley, and yet I had never heard them fight. There was no recollection of fighting at this *shiva*, just a sharing of tears, hugs and laughter as we relived some of the special moments.

CHAPTER THREE

DADDY

The week of *shiva* ended. No more visitors. I went back to work. My father was left alone. My sister and I worried: How would he ever manage without Mommy? She had been his whole life, his reason for being. They had done everything together and she had always taken care of all of the household chores for him. His Parkinson's had gotten so bad that he could not write at all with his left hand and his right hand was beginning to shake. His only desire was to stay in his own house where he could still feel my mother's presence. He stated over and over, "When I can't live alone anymore, I will go to a nursing home. I do not want to be a burden on my children."

Taking care of his family was of utmost importance to my father. He started to plan for the possibility of living in a nursing home. He went to see an elder law attorney so that he could protect some of his assets.

It was hard for him to accept help from me, but he really had no choice. I became a signatory on all of his bank accounts so that I could pay his bills, make deposits and cash his checks. I tried to get to his house at least once a week to help out with mundane matters such as answering his mail, opening up jars and changing the light bulbs.

My father was angry with God for taking away his beloved wife. He said that he would never go to a Rosh Hashana service again. He couldn't bear the thought that God had not inscribed my mother in the Book of Life for that last Rosh Hashana. The words from the prayer book haunted him—

"On Rosh Hashana will be inscribed and on Yom Kippur will be sealed how many will pass from the earth and how many will be created; who will live and who will die; who will die at his predestined time and who before his time; who by water and who by fire, who by sword and who by beast, who by famine and who by thirst, who by storm and who by plague, who by strangulation and who by stoning. Who will rest, and who

will wander, who will live in harmony and who will be harried, who will enjoy tranquility and who will suffer, who will be impoverished and who will be enriched, who will be degraded and who will be exalted. But repentance, prayer and charity remove the evil of the decree."

It was only later that I learned that when the Sages spoke of "life" and "death" it did not necessarily mean our physical existence in this world. Punishments such as plagues and poverty are considered to be "death," while meriting reward is considered "life." Life can also refer to eternal life in the World to Come.

But I didn't know all of this then. I also do not know if my father would have found comfort in this knowledge. It seemed that I was helpless to help him. My father continued to decline, both emotionally and physically. He was once again admitted to the psychiatric ward at the hospital for his depression.

My father didn't want anyone to come to see him except for my sister and me. I went to visit him as often as I could. When it was absolutely necessary, Bob would go to discuss my father's accounting clients with him since Bob was trying to take care of my father's clients in his absence.

My father felt so desperate that he decided to try shock therapy, but I feel these treatments only made his Parkinson's disease worse. When he left the hospital, he was in no condition to go home, so he came to live with us. He was still depressed, and his tremors prevented him from doing almost anything for himself. Some days he was all right. Other times he lay in bed crying all day.

How do you listen to your strong, dependable father sit and cry like a baby all day? How do you deal with having to take care of the person who always took care of you?

BEING CODEPENDENT

I tried to take care of my father and daughter while also juggling visits to my grandmother and my cousin Ezra, who was in a nursing home. This was when I started becoming totally codependent, so consumed by taking care of others that I became physically and emotionally unable to take care of myself.

I always felt torn, never knowing what to do first. It was hard to leave the house because I felt I had to be there to make breakfast, lunch and dinner for my father, who needed so much help, as well as for my husband and daughter. Then there were doctor appointments to arrange and to transport my father to. I tried to spend time with my daughter Ilana, drive her to see friends and help her get ready for school. My husband's business was in the house, so I tried to help him too, in between fixing meals, doing laundry, cleaning up the house and shopping for groceries. Since my father and Aunt Annette were both sick, my grandmother was not getting many visitors. So, I tried to get into Manhattan to see her as often as I could. I had a part-time job and was trying to get a better position.

So what to do first? I would go to the city to see my grandmother and worry that I would not get home in time for my daughter. I would help my husband and worry about the housework that needed to be done. I would do housework and worry about my cousin Ezra who needed a visit. I would visit the nursing home and be upset that I hadn't updated my resume for my job search. Whatever I was doing, I would feel guilty about what I was not doing.

Physically, I was also a mess. Imagine getting stomach pains that would last six to ten hours, once or twice a month, sometimes for two days in a row. Pain so severe that all you could do was sit with a hot water bottle and wait. No medication worked. I just had to wait out the time and eventually the pain would subside. I needed to make a doctor's appointment for myself, but I was so stuck in my codependent role that I could not find any time to arrange it. There was too much to do, so much to take care of already.

I couldn't see my own problems. I thought I was supposed to be the good one, and help others. My misunderstanding of Jewish principles of loving-kindness made it even worse. I was very attracted to all of the biblical role models like our patriarch Abraham, whose tent was open on all sides in order to welcome guests. When God had informed Abraham that He was about to destroy the evil cities of Sodom and Gomorrah, Abraham pleaded with God to save the cities if ten good people could be found there. Then there was our matriarch Rebecca, who I looked up to as a role model. When Eliezer came to her city, she not only gave water to him but she also watered his camels. I was probably most impressed by the way Rachel would have given up the man she loved to spare her older sister the embarrassment of not being the first to be married.

I totally missed the examples of strength and restraint that were necessary for complete faith and devotion to God. I did not understand that kindness is not just something to be extended to others, but that it also needs to be directed toward oneself, and that boundless giving can be both depleting and suffocating. I also did not understand that sometimes strength is what's called for, and not kindness alone. Abraham was willing to sacrifice his son because God had commanded him to do so, even thought it went against his own natural compassion and his love for his son. Our matriarch Sarah spoke to Abraham about sending away Hagar and Ishmael because they would exert a negative influence on Isaac. Jacob parted ways from his brother

Esau when he returned to his homeland because he knew that it would not be good for his family to travel with an evil person. Moses and Aaron went against the Egyptian Pharaoh and later stood up against the Israelites when they wavered from God's way. Sometimes a person has to speak out for what is right even if it does not make that person beloved in the other's eyes.

I wasn't particularly attached to these examples. I hardly noticed them at the time. I had to learn about the importance of acting with strength and restraint, and to act and speak out in accordance with God's will even when faced with obstacles. I needed to learn how to practice kindness toward myself as well as toward my family. Everyone needs a little help now and then. I got some from a teacher, my friend and advisor Dr. Blema Feinstein, who recommended that I go to Codependents Anonymous meetings. She even sent me a list of where those meetings were held.

So there I was, an observant Jew, standing in front of the building. Do I go in to the Codependents Anonymous meeting? Maybe it's not for me! I'm not a, what did she call me, a codependent!

I went in. That didn't help much. There I was looking over this room of strangers and thought, "These people are going to help me? They don't look so special."

I felt awkward and fearful, but I was desperate. I

was sick physically and always felt tired and irritable. It seemed like I never had enough patience with my daughter and was always feeling angry. I know that some people are content with being depressed and unhappy, but I was not. I think I always had a strong desire to find a peaceful, satisfied state of mind. But at this point, I wasn't even close.

The meetings and the twelve-step program of recovery set me on the road to both mental and physical health. I went each week. At first, I didn't tell anyone where I was going. But I kept going. I listened to other people tell their stories. I thanked God that my story didn't seem as bad as theirs. I heard stories of alcoholic spouses and abusive family members. I heard about children who were addicted to drugs or gambling. I heard about people whose children were so abusive and harmful that they had to lock them out of their homes.

My codependency was a learned, addictive, unhealthy behavior. One advantage I had was that I had the wisdom of my heritage on my side. As I learned about what behavior was healthy and what was not, I came to realize that the Torah had been telling me the same thing. I just had not recognized it. The Twelve Steps organized these ideas in a way that I could understand and work on them. I made great progress toward being healthier. However, it was still a slow process. I had developed bad habits over my entire lifetime, now

I would have the rest of my life to develop healthy ones.

My father really wanted to leave my house and go home, but he needed to learn how to function in his disabled state. So I made an appointment for him with an occupational therapist. Thank God we found a wonderful therapist who was also determined to help him return home. I drove him to his first appointment. Then he began to drive himself. Driving gave my father back his much-needed independence. (As his condition deteriorated, this was one of the last things he gave up.) Although he would later limit himself to only local excursions, at that time he was still able to drive the ninety miles or so to my sister's house.

Daddy stayed with us for about nine months. Then he returned to his own home. His life revolved around helping his children and grandchildren and being in his own home, surrounded by the memories of my mother. He occasionally visited with his friends. They were all wonderful, inviting him to visit and to join them at dinner. As his disease progressed, he saw these friends less and less, and eventually went out to dinner only with the family. Each Friday he would come to my house for Shabbat dinner.

Daddy tried to make up for the loss of Mommy. I came over and marked his calendar with all of the birthdays and anniversaries so that he could send cards to everyone on time. He took all of his granddaughters shopping for clothes before school started, since this had been something that Mommy had done. Two of my nieces were in the Broadway show *Joseph*, and he became their chaperone, driving to Westchester, going back and forth with them on the bus and then returning to Long Island. He actually talked to all of us on the phone since he could no longer hand the phone over to my mother, as he used to do when she was alive. We were now able to build a wonderful relationship with a father who had never really talked too much to us before.

This was the strong, dependable Daddy that I had always remembered. But this Daddy also needed help. Our friend Lori cleaned for him every other week and he looked forward to the days that she came. He would often extend the day by taking her out for lunch. I continued to go to his house once a week to pay his bills, answer any correspondence, change light bulbs and open jars — all of which provided me with a good excuse to check up on him and spend some time together.

I also kept going to meetings and started to take better care of myself. I finally went to a gastroenterologist for my stomach problems. When he could not find a reason or offer a solution, I put myself on the "fit for life" diet. I eventually went back to studying Torah with my friends, something that I had neglected for what I thought was a lack of time. Then when I turned forty, I enrolled in a martial arts program and began looking into the compatibility of the Twelve Steps and Codependence Anonymous meetings with Torah. This investigation would lead four and a half years later to my first book, *Starting Over*. I also realized that no matter how hard I tried, I just was not going to get a decent job in teaching. So I changed direction, and took a part-time position as a recreation therapist at the Long Island State Veterans Home in Stony Brook. Since the job was only twenty hours a week and five minutes away from my house, I still had time to write, take care of my household, tend to my father and continue to try to make myself healthy.

As my health improved, my father's health deteriorated. Driving became more difficult for him. He stopped going to my sister's house and to my grandmother's apartment in the city. I had to drive him to his appointments with the neurologist in Queens. Eventually, I would also have to drive him to his doctor appointments in his area. He always kept his sense of humor, but he also kept his subscription to the Hemlock Society, the organization that advocates suicide when a person feels he no longer wants to live. I would argue with my father about the issue of suicide. I used to warn him, "If you want to be with Mommy some day, then you can't do this. You'll blow it. She will be in one place and you will be in another!" I couldn't think of any other threat that would affect him. But his physical decline was soon to make the threat of suicide irrelevant.

We began to worry about his safety. We tried to convince him to give up his upstairs bedroom and move downstairs or maybe get an elevator installed. But my father was stubborn. He did not want to waste the money and he reiterated that when he couldn't manage, he would move to a nursing home. We wanted him to get one of those medical alert devices that he could press if he was in trouble. He wouldn't hear of it. So we simply tried to watch over him from a distance, as best as we could. I learned that you cannot give to someone what they are not able to receive.

CHAPTER FOUR

HARRY

Just as I was getting pretty good at balancing all of my responsibilities, we found out that Bob's father, Harry, had suffered a heart attack and was hospitalized in Florida. Harry was one of the kindest people I knew, easy going and patient. Bob's mother, Lilly, was the tough one.

I remember the first night Bob brought me to his parents' house. He told me to go downstairs in the den and wait for him there. While I was waiting, Lilly came to the den to see me.

"What are you doing here?" she asked.

"Bob told me to wait here for him," I replied.

"You listen to men? I never listen to men," she exclaimed.

That was my introduction to my future mother-in-law Lilly, but no matter how exasperating she was, I always felt accepted by her. And no matter what she said or did, I never heard Harry complain about her.

Of course, Bob's family was not exactly like mine. My family, unlike Bob's, was more of the picture-perfect "Father knows best" type of family that routinely ate their meals together. Harry, Bob's father, owned a bakery and made the best Russian coffee cake that I ever tasted. I would often meet Bob at his parents' house after work. Harry, who arrived at the bakery at 2:00 in the morning, went home earlier than Lilly, who stayed until closing at 6:00 p.m. The memory of one of those nights sticks in my mind. Harry was the only one there when I arrived and the conversation went something like this:

"Sit down. We'll eat dinner."

"Shouldn't we wait for Bob and Lilly?"

"What for?"

So, we sat and ate. Harry was often the cook in the house. And Bob and his mother ate whenever they arrived later.

Harry and Lilly were always there when Bob and I needed them. Once my car broke down on the highway, and they came to the gas station to retrieve me and all of the purchases I had just made, including a rather large rug, which, if I recall correctly, I later returned.

They were always there, even when we didn't need them. I was in labor for twenty-two hours with our daughter Ilana. When they arrived unexpectedly, Bob had to send them home. Ilana would not be born until the next day.

Even before Ilana was born, it became more difficult for them to run the bakery. So they sold it. As they got older, it became harder for them to take care of their house. The grass needed to be mowed in the summer and the snow needed to be shoveled in the winter. So Harry and Lilly decided to move to Florida.

Ilana was about four at the time. Our vacations became Florida vacations, as Harry and Lilly became long-distance grandparents. Trips to DisneyWorld and the Kennedy Space Center. Driving to Florida in December and taking off a layer of clothing at each rest stop. Ilana's excitement in the plane as she watched the puffy clouds out the window. Airboats, swamps and alligators.

And Century Village with all of their rules. No children in the clubhouse. Heat the pool? What for? We don't swim here in the winter! Out of the pool! It's time for lunch. Out of the pool! It's time for dinner. Early bird specials. What do you mean we have to drive thirty miles for a kosher restaurant? Park only in the designated visitor spots.

Lilly seemed to mellow in Florida, and then she got sick. Harry, the dutiful husband, the man who did whatever had to be done, took care of her. Harry, the veteran of World War II, who told me that he used to cook for the soldiers and search through the villages to find fresh eggs and potatoes for the men. Harry, the man who stood by his mother and sister when his own father deserted the family. Harry, who called my daughter the baby no matter how old she got, who took her to play shuffle board and painted pictures with her in his spare time. He cooked, he cleaned, he took care of the laundry. He drove Lilly wherever she needed to go, for shopping and to the doctors. He gave her insulin shots for her diabetes and got up with her in the middle of the night when she needed his help. And through all of this I never once heard him complain.

But now Lilly was sick. And that meant extra trips to Florida for Bob, and for his sister Andrea and his brother Jerry. They tried to set up home health care for Harry and Lilly but it never seemed to last for too long. I wouldn't understand how difficult it was to organize and keep home health services until I would later have to do the same at my house for my grandmother.

They also tried to conserve some of Harry and Lilly's assets in the event that she would need long-term care in a nursing home. Bob, Jerry and Andrea contacted an elder law attorney who helped to set up the wills, trusts and gift allocations in order to meet Medicaid eligibility.

Lilly didn't last long enough to need our plans for Medicaid. She got worse, but Harry continued to care for her, mostly by himself. I still never heard him complain. Eventually, she had a series of strokes and needed to be admitted to a nursing home.

It's a funny thing. We human beings can be so self-assured. We think that we are so scientifically advanced, that we know so much. At one point we were told that Lilly had been declared brain dead. But not long after, we got a phone call and it was Lilly, in person, talking on the phone to Bob, asking him to come to Florida. So now it was one more trip for Bob to Florida, and then his mother was gone.

Taking care of Lilly had taken its toll on Harry. He already had high blood pressure and a bad heart. Shortly after Lilly's death, he, too, began to fail. We knew that he was on borrowed time. In December of 1996 Bob's brother and sister made a visit to Florida. By then, Harry was in a nursing home due to congestive heart failure. I could not take off from work, so Bob took Ilana out of school and together they went to see Harry. Bob was worried that this might be their last chance to see him.

I got a phone call.

"Harry is better and they want to discharge him from the nursing home, but he can't go home alone. Should I bring him back to stay with us?" Bob asked tentatively.

What a question for a codependent, a person who is addicted to taking care of others! But I was a recovering codependent. I knew now that I needed to evaluate the situation, ask myself certain questions and then make a choice.

Does he really need to leave his home and live with one of his children?

Yes.

Can Bob's brother or sister take him in?

No.

Our home and lifestyle were uniquely suited to looking after Harry. I worked part-time, five minutes from the house. Bob's business was run from the house itself, and he made his own schedule to see clients. We could also rely on two special trustworthy friends. Even Ilana was old enough to "grandpa sit," if we needed her. With a little coordination, someone could always be at the house with Harry.

But what about my codependent tendency to get swallowed up in the care of others?

This would be my challenge. But I would not try to do everything myself. I would continue to go to CoDA meetings so that I wouldn't slip back into unhealthy

habits. Jerry and Andrea would also help out occasionally by visiting and taking him to their homes for visits.

What impact, I wondered, would this have on
Ilana?

She was older at this point. As an only child, Ilana
was not used to sharing her parents or her space with
others. Maybe, in the long run, this would be a good
experience for her, even if it was a difficult one.

And what about Harry himself?

Of all of the grandparents, Harry had the easiest
nature. He was never demanding or complaining. I also
knew that Harry had taken care of people his whole life.
He certainly deserved to have someone take care of him.

My answer?

"Bring him home. We will do it for as long as we
can."

So the balancing act began. I continued to work as
a recreational therapist twenty hours a week. Bob was
about to begin the busy tax season. My father's
Parkinson's was also beginning to get worse.

It was hard for Ilana. When my father had lived
with us, he was depressed and mostly stayed in his bedroom upstairs. We were only too happy when he came
out of the bedroom to join us for a meal. But unlike my
father, Harry couldn't make the stairs, so Bob and I
moved upstairs and left Harry downstairs in the bedroom adjacent to Ilana's room. Most of the time, he

would stay in the living room watching television, space that Ilana was accustomed to having for herself. The hardest night was Friday night when Ilana had to deal with all us adults — two parents and two grandpas, as my father continued to come to our house for Shabbat dinner. It became easier for her when she invited a friend to join us.

With Bob busy working, I tried to spend as much time as I could with Harry. I would fold the laundry in the living room so that we could chat. When Harry first arrived, he would help me. Later on, he would just keep me company. Being a baker, he gave me some good tips on baking *challah* bread. I think he was proud of my Friday-night breads.

I was careful with Harry's diet. We all got used to eating salt-free foods. Even the *challahs* were low-salt. I made special low-salt, healthy lunches for the days when it was just Harry and me at home. However, I must admit that Harry's favorite lunches were when he went out to lunch with one of his children, unhealthy food and all.

Bob went out with him as often as he could, giving me some time alone with Ilana, and Jerry and Andrea would visit on the weekends, sometimes with their spouses. The liveliest visitor was Jerry and Susan's daughter Kami. She was a very active two-year-old at the time. Like most old people, Harry loved to see this very energetic and loving granddaughter of his. However, he also found her exhausting just to watch. Occasionally, Harry went to their home to visit for a few days.

I was still going to my father's house to help him all the while I was looking after Harry and also trying to save some time and energy for my daughter when she got home from school. Then there was still Mom and cousin Ezra to visit. Mom was getting more and more confused. The social worker wanted her to accept more help in the house but she still refused. Poor Ezra. He always got shortchanged. I just didn't have so many extra days to fit him in. I went when I could.

So the months passed. I juggled things and managed as best as I could to do most of the things that had to get done.

CHAPTER FIVE

A PARTY *and a* DOWNHILL SLIDE

❧

Harry had arrived in December. Ilana was going to be twelve in May and we were planning a party for her *Bat Mitzvah*. Each time I visited Mom, she would give me a check for Ilana. She said, "In case I don't make it to the *Bat Mitzvah* party." I would say, "Mom, don't worry. You'll make it to the party." But she was not convinced, so she would periodically tell me to make a check out to Ilana, just in case.

Thank God, she did make it to the party. So did Harry and my father. It was wonderful. We were dancing to Jewish music and my niece Rebecca went to get

Mom up from her chair. We didn't think she would join us, but then there she was, dancing with all of us. I went into the center of the circle with her and held her hands. Slowly around and around we danced. Then my sister Valerie joined us—just the grandma and her two grand-daughters. What a joyous time! Then her great-grand-daughters and my cousin Vicki joined in. Soon all of the women were clapping and dancing.

My father had a great time at the party, and there was Harry, who we never thought would make it to the spring. He was so proud of Ilana but it had been a diffi-cult day for him. He got very tired at the *Bat Mitzvah*, so I left the party early to take him home.

Everyone's health seemed to deteriorate that sum-mer. Harry slept more and more and went out less and less. Mom was getting more and more frightened about living in her apartment. I spoke to her almost every day and tried to get to see her at least once a month. She kept telling me about people that she said were breaking into her apartment and stealing from her. The social worker from her building was pressuring us to arrange more help, but Mom was very strong about not wanting strangers in her house. I took her to see a neuropsychol-ogist. She prescribed medication and suggested further testing. Mom started wandering out of her apartment in the middle of the night. She never seemed to know what time it was. She would nap during the day and wake up thinking it was morning when it was evening. Mom had reached ninety-one-years old. We decided not to subject her to a battery of tests.

Meanwhile, my father's Parkinson's was getting worse. He began to experience weakness in his feet. He had always walked a few miles around his condo complex each day. Now, when he tried to walk, he would have to sit on the curb when his legs gave out. Eventually the walks got shorter and shorter. He no longer came over for Shabbat dinners.

It was about this time that my father went to see an elder law attorney. He figured that he was going to end up in a nursing home. Like Harry and Lilly, he wanted to protect some of his assets for his children and grandchildren. The lawyer was impressed by my father's concern for his family and his trust in my sister and me. I was not surprised. My father had always been extremely generous to both family and friends.

Harry was also getting weaker. It was getting hard for Harry to physically take care of himself. The doctor prescribed a wheelchair and kept telling us to call the hospice program. We also didn't quite understand at the time that hospice meant less than six months left to live. We decided it was time, perhaps overdue, to arrange for some home health care. We applied to Medicare for a home health aide.

I remember the day the aide came. What a nice

young man he was. He bathed Harry, cleaned his room and scrubbed the bathroom until it was spotless. He was so kind that Harry didn't mind his help. He would be back again in two days. That was the plan.

The next day, Bob's brother, Jerry, came out to visit with Harry. It was a warm August day, but Harry felt cold. This was not unusual. I don't think he ever readjusted to New York weather after Florida. We were sitting in the kitchen and I suggested that Harry go in the backyard to warm up in the sun. We have a sliding glass door from the kitchen, so he did not have far to go. We brought him outside in his new wheelchair and gave him a newspaper to read. We were hot, so we all stayed in the kitchen where we could stay cool and still see him. All of a sudden, he slumped forward. We ran out-side to get him. He was disoriented. He talked about being in Czechoslovakia. Bob and Jerry helped him into bed. We didn't know what to do. Should we bring him to the hospital? Should we give it some time and see what happens?

The boys went for a walk to talk matters over and to try and figure out what to do. I sat in the bedroom with Harry. He seemed to be having pain in his head. I took his hand, and then to my surprise, he started to pat my hand. He was suffering, and yet he was trying to comfort me.

The decision was made to take him to the hospital

because of the pain, even if we weren't sure about the rest of his condition. Bob and Jerry got him into the car somehow and drove away. Ilana was at a friend's house, and I was alone. The house was suddenly quiet. I remember feeling so tired. There was nothing to do but rest and wait for everyone to return. That was the last time I would see Harry.

Bob later told me that Harry was disoriented at the hospital. First the nurse in the emergency room asked him some questions.

"Mr. Schloss, do you know where you are?" the nurse inquired.

"Yes," Harry replied. "I'm in ice cream heaven."

Later the doctor continued the conversation.

"Mr. Schloss, do you know where you are?"

"Yes," Harry replied. "I'm in the hospital."

"Do you know where the hospital is?" the doctor continued.

"On a hill," Harry answered.

"Where is the hill?" the doctor persisted.

"In Czechoslovakia," Harry answered.

Bob continued the conversation.

"Dad, how could we be in Czechoslovakia?"

"I don't know."

"Do you remember driving here in your car?"

"Yes."

"Do you remember leaving from my house in

Stony Brook?"

"Yes."

"You know you can't drive from my house to Czechoslovakia."

"I know."

"So how did we get here?"

"I don't know, but we're in Czechoslovakia."

Bob returned home that evening. Harry was admitted to the hospital. He seemed to be recovering. Karen, Bob's associate and our friend, went to see him in the hospital. She met with the doctor who told her that Harry was doing much better. On Monday morning I brought an application in to the Long Island State Veterans Home. We thought how nice it was that he was a veteran, so if he had to be in a nursing home at least he would be at the facility where I worked. I would be able to visit him every day that I worked. The Veterans Home was only a five-minute drive from the house so Bob could also visit whenever he wanted, and if Harry felt up to it, we could even bring him home for a visit. It was a really good place for veterans, with a feeling of camaraderie. I would introduce him to all of the guys. He'd have friends in no time.

As fate would have it, none of my plans for Harry were meant to be. In Yiddish there is an expression that roughly translated means, "Man plans and God laughs." Why do we humans love to plan so much for the future? Why are we so surprised when our plans fall through? Why do we act as if this physical life could last forever?

Ilana came home from school on Monday afternoon and told Bob that she wanted to go see her grandfather at the hospital. What urged her to go? It would turn out to be a blessing that they went.

I got home from work at about 10:00 p.m. Bob and Ilana told me that they had a wonderful visit. Harry was feeling good. They kissed him goodnight and Bob promised to return the next day. The doctor said that he was doing amazingly well.

We got the call about 1:00 a.m. Harry had been up watching late-night TV when he told the nursing staff that he was tired and wanted to go to bed. They helped him into bed. He closed his eyes, and he was gone.

Bob went to the hospital. I got on the phone with the funeral home. Bob decided that the funeral would be that afternoon since the next day meant more than twenty-four hours. He felt that since the immediate family was local, there was no need to delay it for the few people who might not be able to make it. Jewish law states that a funeral should take place within twenty-four hours when possible. Experience had taught us that it is also the best possible plan. Waiting for my mother's funeral had been a terrible ordeal.

I guess that I have become the family memorial

service speaker. I spoke about what a wonderful person Harry was. Ilana also spoke some beautiful words about her grandfather. Then we returned to the little cemetery where Lilly was buried. We continued the practice of filling in the whole grave, and we had lots of help from my sister's family. A cousin then remembered that he was a *Cohen*, a descendant of Aaron, the priestly family that served in the Temple in Jerusalem. According to Jewish law, *Cohanim* are not permitted to go to the cemetery. Aside from the humor of this non-practicing Jew "remembering" his priestly status at a most opportune moment, it struck me that it is pretty amazing to realize that, even after thousands of years, Jews still know if they are Levites or *Cohanim*.

We were back to the house now for another *shiva*. My mother had been the first. Lilly, the second. Now Harry was the third. Again a crowd of people on the first day, and then, for the most part, they were gone.

There were already so many people missing who had been part of the previous *shiva*. Both of our mothers and my Aunt Shirley were gone. My father was not doing so well and could only drive short distances. This time I was the one to get the bagels and rolls for the morning *minyanim*. Getting the worshippers together was harder without my father's condo friends who had been there for my father when my mother had passed away. We managed. We didn't know it at the time, but we were about to have a very busy year ahead of us.

THE CONTINUING DECLINE

It seemed like all of the older generation was either gone or failing. Aunt Annette had missed the party for Ilana's *Bat Mitzvah* because she was sick again. Her cancer was back, and by the fall she was back in the hospital. My father was having trouble walking and doing things for himself. My grandmother was getting more and more confused.

However, for a change I was now a little healthier. I knew that I had to take care of myself if I was to be there for all of the people who needed me. Part of taking care of myself was finding outside help for my father. The home health aide had come too late for Harry. I did not want to make the same mistake again. Medicare would provide four hours of help a day for five days a week. The agency sent us a woman named Innocile. Or perhaps I should say that through the agency, God sent us Innocile. I still went over to check on Daddy and to pay his bills, but Innocile did the cooking, cleaned, did the laundry, shopped and provided him with daily companionship.

One day, I couldn't get through to him on the phone. I assumed that he had gone out shopping with

Innocile. She had gone to his house and rang the door bell. When he did not answer, she assumed that he was with me. I finally got through around 3:00 p.m.

"Sheila, come over. (He always called me by my English name.) I fell down in the bathroom this morning. I couldn't get out for seven hours." Of course, I went dashing over there, filled with remorse for not checking on him sooner. He had somehow made it to the bed. There was blood on the bathroom floor and on his bedroom carpet. He had bruised himself, but nothing was broken. He was badly shaken. I could only imagine what it was like, trying to get up only to fall again; and then finally summoning enough strength after seven long hours to crawl out of the room and over to a phone.

"Daddy, you have to get one of those beepers so you can just press the button if you are in trouble," I begged him.

"Okay. I'll wear a beeper. Whatever you say, " he replied. At this point he was too tired to argue.

So we arranged for him to wear a wristband with a button to press. A callbox was placed in his bedroom. If he pressed the button and did not answer when they called, then the company would automatically call me. In addition, we gave them two other phone numbers to call if I could not be reached. In this way we felt a little more secure about him living alone. This is what he wanted more than anything else, to live in his home where he could still feel my mother's presence for as long as he possibly could.

CHAPTER SIX

MOM
MOVES IN

Mom was alone and in need of more help. My father could no longer drive to see her. My Aunt Annette remained in the hospital. I tried to get into the city as often as I could. Sometimes I took Mom to the hospital to see Aunt Annette.

Aunt Annette was failing physically, and Mom was failing mentally. The social worker told me that she would wander around the building in the middle of the night. She would talk to her "friend" in the mirror and then go to the lobby to meet her. Of course, the "friend" never showed up.

So it was arranged that Mom would have an aide come in for seven hours a day, except on weekends. The social worker wanted her to have more help in the house, but Mom refused. She was too frightened of all of the people that she already imagined were breaking into her house. "No more strangers," she continued to insist. When the agency sent someone anyway, she would lock her door and refuse to let her in.

Then she started losing her keys. She would go for days, unable to leave the house because she had no key for the door. I kept making new keys for her, and she kept losing them.

I knew that Aunt Annette was dying. I couldn't imagine how Mom would survive alone once her faithful daughter, who had always looked after her, passed away. So I tried again.

"Mom, maybe you should come live with me?"

"Yes. You're right."

Yes? She actually said yes? I had been trying to get her to move in with us for years. My ever cautious husband thought that we should have a trial period to make sure she would be happy living with us. She could just pack a bag and try it out for a week or two. I made the suggestion to Mom.

"I can't go without my things," was her reply.

"Well, what if you hate living with us. Once you close up the apartment, you won't be able to move back in," I tried to reason.

"What's there to hate?" she replied. "Will you starve me? Throw me into the street?"

"Of course not."

"So I'll be happy there."

"But maybe you should try it anyway. Then we can move your stuff later."

"We can't do that."

"Why not?"

"Everything will be gone. They'll steal it. There won't be anything left."

Mom's mind was made up. She would come, but only if she could bring all of her things along. She had always been very strong-willed and steadfast. When she made up her mind, that was it. So what could I do? I hired a mover and moved all of her things.

Our house was small. Where we were going to put all of her things was not exactly clear. My living room couch was old, so I decided to throw it out and put hers in instead. Bob and I moved upstairs and gave her our bedroom but it only fit one of her twin beds. How can you break up twins? So my sister Valerie took the other one. Her breakfront was in competition with my wall unit. So the breakfront went into her bedroom. She could not understand why I did not want it in my living room. It was a classic—a replica of one that was shown in the 1939 New York World's Fair, as noted by a metal plate inside one of the drawers. Still, I guess that I could be pretty strong-willed too. I was not ready to give up the wall unit that I had purchased during the first year of my marriage.

Having learned that I could not take care of someone in my home all by myself, I arranged for a home health care aide to start the same week that Mom moved in. It wasn't easy though. I tried to get someone to come during the twenty hours that I worked, with some additional hours to give me a break when I was home. Aides came and went. Mom was a tough customer and rejected many of them. She would say, "What good are they if they have to ask me what they need to do? They should know what to do!" Just when things seemed to be working out, the Social Services switched us to another program, which meant we could not even use the same agency any longer. So we had to begin the whole process of trying out new people all over again. It was difficult, but I did not give up. I knew that the only way this could work would be if we had some help in the house.

JUST IN TIME

Mom's move came at the end of November. I had hoped that she would be with me before Aunt Annette passed away. Meanwhile, my father's condition was rapidly deteriorating. He could barely climb the stairs, and after much coaxing, we finally had his bed moved downstairs into his living room. The only time he would go up was to shower and only when someone was in the house with him. Besides all this, his thumb kept slipping behind his pointer finger. It would get stuck there and cause him great pain. So he began to call us at all hours, sometimes late at night, and either Bob or I would have to drive over to his house to adjust the position of his thumb.

Then something happened that we will never understand. He suddenly started to suffer from excruciating pain. All kinds of medication were tried, even some very powerful drugs that were prescribed by his neurologist, but nothing seemed to relieve the agony. He could barely move, and now he spent most of the day in bed. He talked only of his wish to die.

I went to his house and said, "You can't go on like this. Let's go to the hospital." So I drove him to the hospital, where they gave him a shot that seemed to relieve the pain. Back home he seemed okay for a day, but then the pain returned, and so did his desire to die. Innocile stayed the night. Fearful that he might start the car in the garage and sit in it until he died, Innocile took his keys and hid them. The social worker wanted to send in a crisis team. They told me not to go over. They would convince him to go to a psychiatric hospital. I might get in the way. The hours flew by, and they still hadn't shown up. Innocile was still with him, but we were all feeling rather apprehensive. My father was still in terrible pain.

Right or wrong I felt that we couldn't wait any longer. I knew that my father usually listened to me and at least considered my suggestions. I arrived at the house and saw him writhing in pain. Innocile had to go home. Shabbat and the weekend were fast approaching. I tried to call his local doctor. He was not available.

I said, "Daddy, you can't go on like this."

He replied, "What should I do?"

"I'm going to take you back to the hospital."

"Whatever you think."

The hospital had both a pain clinic and a psychiatric unit. His doctor could not be reached, and so there was a long delay in admitting him. As Shabbat approached, I began to get nervous. My husband calmed me over the telephone. "You have no choice, this has to be done."

I think that it was after midnight when he finally was admitted. I wish I could say that this story had a happy ending. It didn't. The pain clinic tried many procedures, but they could never find the source of his pain or a solution for it.

He was so frightened. I tried to be with him each

time they tried something new. Then there was another procedure for which they told me to wait outside. After this he asked if my friend Jeff Goldstein, an anesthesiologist at the hospital, could be with him if the family could not. It was too hard for him to face these frightening procedures alone.

I watched my father fade away day after day. My strong, supportive, intelligent father now seemed so fragile and helpless. I thought of how I had been angry and had blamed him when my mother died. Why had he had that mental breakdown when she was sick? Why had she depleted her limited strength supporting his emotional weakness? As I watched him suffer my anger melted away. Who was I to judge? And if he was in anyway responsible for my mother, it was now he who was suffering ten times over.

I kept thinking of my mother. I had prayed that she should live. My father told me later that he had prayed that she should not have any pain. Cancer patients usually suffer in enormous pain. Not my mother. Even the last night of her life we asked her, "Do you need anything for the pain?" "No" was her simple reply. It seemed to me that my father had somehow taken all of her pain upon himself, and now, in one month, he had all the pain that she would have had to endure in the two years that she was sick.

My father was dying. I asked the doctor. "What is

happening here? You can't die from pain!" The doctor's reply was: "I would call this a failure to thrive." We called the hospice. We tried to prepare ourselves.

People who work with the sick and dying know about the importance of humor. Perhaps it reminds us that we should not take anything in life too seriously. Somehow humor is cleansing and purifying. It can give us the strength to continue on in this crazy world. In any condition, my father would never lose an opportunity to look at the lighter side.

My father had a dry sense of humor. I thought about how he had made us laugh in the past. When I graduated from high school and everyone was walking so seriously down the aisle in their caps and gowns, I suddenly heard a voice. As I passed my parents, I could hear my father saying, "Here comes the judge. Here comes the judge."

So his first encounter with a nurse from hospice came as no surprise to me, although it may have shocked her. My father was lying in the bed, so weak that he could barely move or talk. The hospice nurse spoke in a loud voice, as do many people who speak to patients who seem non-responsive.

"How do you feel, Mr. Kesselman?" she asked in a loud voice.

"With my hands," he simply replied.

I wish I had a camera to capture the reaction.

"Did he say with his hands?" she asked me.

"He certainly did," I answered in between my laughter.

Another time he made us laugh and I don't think he even knew it. He was hallucinating from some of the pain medication. We got a late-night call from a nurse on his unit. He had insisted that she call us.

"Does your father own this hospital?" the nurse asked with a worried expression.

"No," I replied.

"Well, maybe you'd better talk to him."

So she put him on the phone.

"It's no good. We've got to sell the hospital. They're all a bunch of crooks. It isn't worth anything anymore," my father ranted.

I don't even remember how I answered him but I somehow reassured her that we didn't own the hospital. I asked the nurse if she wanted me to come to the hospital.

"No," she replied. "I'll try to calm him down. I'll call you if I need you."

Well, did we laugh. Imagine, my father had convinced the nurse that he actually owned the hospital. Bob said we should have played along. Then he would have really gotten the best of care!

But the days of laughter were soon replaced with days of tears. My father got so weak that he could not eat even if he wanted to. We tried to get him to drink.

Then, in the last days of December, he drank a little bit of liquid food supplement. Bob said that he was holding out for the new year because he knew it would be better for his final tax return.

January arrived. Maybe Bob was right. My father could no longer swallow. We put drops of water into his mouth to relieve the dryness. He had insisted on no artificial life support, including IV or feeding tubes. So there was nothing we could do but visit each day and watch him fade away.

Bob and I went to see him on Saturday night, January 3, after Shabbat. I was afraid to leave the hospital. What if he died? I did not want him to die alone. Around 11:00 p.m., I called the hospice care. A hospice nurse came over to talk to us. She told us stories of people who had waited for loved ones to arrive before they died and people who had waited for loved ones to leave before they died. It seems that people have some control over the exact moment of their death, over the point of letting go.

The hospice nurse stayed for about an hour with us and I was finally convinced that I could go home. My father's death would be between my father and God. I would accept whatever happened.

I went to work on Sunday. My sister went to the hospital. It was a long trip for her, and so she also had to face the awful decision of when to come and how long to stay. Monday I went to work, but I knew that I would not be able to stay all day. I got a call from the hospital. My father's death was imminent.

Back to the hospital. My sister was on her way. I kept telling my father, "Valerie is coming. She'll be here soon."

At one point, not even knowing if he could hear me, I cried to my father, "It isn't fair. You didn't even give me a chance to say good-bye." And then my father began to cry. I felt so bad. How could I do this. "I'm sorry Daddy. It's okay. You've been saying good-bye for five years. If it's time to go, it's okay. We'll be all right. We had wonderful times together."

And then I started to talk to him about the wonderful times.

"Remember when we used to go to the Long Island Ducks' hockey games. Sometimes we would yell so much that I would be hoarse the next day. You used to buy tickets on the right side of the arena for me because I insisted that I couldn't see as well from the other side because I was 'right-eyed.'

"You often brought other family members on our vacations. I'm remembering the car trip to Niagara Falls with my cousin Ezra and his wife Bonnie. Every time we passed an information station Ezra would roll down his windows and yell, 'Liars!' We finally made it to the Falls. We all stood by the Falls and were feeling what we thought was mist. The car was parked very far away. By the time we realized that it wasn't just mist it was too late. It was pouring. Everyone ran to the car laughing. We all got soaking wet.

"Laughing. That's what I recall most about our vacations. What we actually saw in each place fades from my memory. But the memory of the fun and laughter remains. The most laughter had to be when we went to Washington D.C. with Mom. Remember when we stayed in that rinky dink motel in Maryland. Valerie, Mom and I shared a room, and we laughed so much that you and Mommy had to tell us to be quiet or they would surely throw us out of the motel."

Valerie finally arrived with Bob and her oldest daughter, Amanda. I told them and the doctor how my father had cried when I told him that he didn't give us a chance to say good-bye. They also agreed that he had been saying good-bye ever since my mother died.

I now saw firsthand how people have some control over the moment of releasing their hold on life. My father hung on the whole time that Amanda and Bob were there. Then they left and it was only Valerie and me. My strong Daddy who had supported us and made us laugh seemed so small and fragile. As it says in Psalms: "a passing shadow." Just like my mother, his breathing got slower and slower until it just stopped. It was very calm and peaceful. I closed his eyes and said,

"Blessed are You, our God, King of the universe, the true judge." I then made a rip in my shirt, known as tearing *kriyah*, as Jewish people do when a close family member dies (a mother, father, sibling, child, or spouse).

While the funeral home attendant ran around trying to get the appropriate papers, my sister and I sat in his hospital room. We waited there for about five hours. Every time the hospital staff said that they wanted to move him to the morgue, we told them that we would wait in the room with his body until the funeral director came to take him. Finally, after several attempts on the hospital staff's part, my sister went out and told them that it was a religious commandment to stay with the body, and as I was religious there was no way that I would let them move the body and leave it unattended. They finally got the message and left us alone.

It may seem strange, but sitting there with my sister was both calming and healing. It was a precious moment when time seemed to keep still. Nothing really mattered. There was no place to go, no errands to run. Just the two of us keeping the mitzvah of watching over our father's body. It was time for us to share our thoughts with each other. Time to be silent, to just be. We left the hospital when the people from the funeral home arrived and then time continued to speed on in its usual manner.

It was the funeral, the week of *shiva* and a whirlwind of people. And then all was quiet again. In keeping with the custom of taking a short walk after the *shiva*, we went once around the block, and it was over.

There is so much wisdom in the Jewish laws of mourning that places limits on a mourner's social interactions. I needed that time and space to renew myself both physically and emotionally.

The sharpness of the loss began to lift a little. Now the pain and the emptiness began to settle in, along with a feeling of complete exhaustion. My inner core of energy was depleted. I could barely make it through each day. The combination of grief and sadness had taken its toll on my physical health. I knew that I had to replenish myself. Increasing vitamins and taking recommended herbs was my first defense against illness. My second defense was being more careful about diet, exercise and getting sufficient rest.

The reality of taking care of mundane matters also settled in. We were still receiving some checks from my father's old office to be paid to the estate of Melvin Kesselman. Although I still had a joint account with him at a local bank, they would not accept checks made out to the estate. In order to deposit or cash those checks, I had to open an estate account. This meant that I had to probate my father's will so that I could receive letters of testamentary declaring my sister and me as co-executrices of his estate, a condition which was required by the bank before they would open an estate account. The forms had to be filed in the Surrogate Court, which was about an hour away. When we approached the elder law attorney to do this for us, he said that he could not give us a flat fee for taking care of this matter and could not even agree to a maximum amount or cap on the total charges. So we decided to try to navigate the courts for ourselves.

The first time I drove to Surrogate Court I made sure that I had all of the necessary documents including a certified copy of my father's will and death certificate. To my horror and amazement, I could not complete the process because the lawyer had neglected to notarize the signatures of the witnesses for the will. I would have to find the witnesses and have them sign another form stating that they had in fact witnessed my father's will, and the statement would have to be notarized.

First I cried because I remembered how I used to bring all of my legal forms to my mother to notarize. She had been a legal secretary, a paralegal and a notary public. So I cried for awhile. My husband quickly reminded me that most banks had at least one notary public on staff. Sometimes what you need is some practical information.

Anxiety began to settle in when I called the lawyer's office only to find out that the two witnesses no longer worked for his firm. The office offered no assistance as to their whereabouts. How would I find them? Since they had left the office only two months earlier, we were lucky enough to find that one of them had a listed telephone number at the same address that was listed in the will. She helped me to find the other witness. Then, with some help from the post office, I got notarized forms back from both of them and then made the trek to Surrogate Court, one more time. Finally, everything was in order and the court issued the necessary letters of testamentary.

We also had to take care of my father's house. This also caused us to run into complications due to paperwork that had not been filed properly with the town. Since the house had originally been in my mother's name, I had to produce a certified copy of her death certificate. This required a trip to the town where I grew up and where my mother passed away. Another day for memories and tears.

In the midst of trying to take care of all of this mundane business, there was still Mom. As the weeks went by, she seemed to fade in and out of reality. I continued to take her to see her daughter, Aunt Annette, who was dying of cancer in a nursing facility. All Mom could say was, "Look how beautiful she looks."

Mom seemed to see what she wanted to see. Perhaps it is a gift. How could she have visited her if she saw the thin, frail figure before her. Maybe it was better this way.

The winter passed. The leaves returned to the trees and the flowers bloomed. My daughter found it harder and harder to share her space with this very demented old lady that she knew as her great-grandmother. I kept saying, "We'll do it for as long as we can." But I was still so tired. After going through so many home health aides we found Lorraine. Finally we had someone reliable who could handle Mom.

But my family was still feeling the pressure. Maybe we needed a break. We took Mom to my sister's house and went up to the Catskills for a few days. We returned and then got the call. Annette had passed away. The funeral would be in a few days. How do we tell Mom? My sister felt it would be better to wait until she returned to my house. Then we would tell her together.

Would she comprehend? Can anyone fully come to terms with the fact that their entire life was gone: Her husband, her children, all of her brothers and sisters. Could we three grandchildren ever fill the void in her life? Somehow I didn't think so.

And what about my cousin Andrew whose mother had died. He was not yet eighteen. How would he be comforted? And how would Uncle Joe who was much older than my Aunt Annette be comforted of the loss of his young wife?

The senior generation was almost all gone. Only

Mom and Uncle Joe remained from my family, and there were two aunts and an uncle on Bob's side. How strange. How lonely. Did this mean that I was now part of the old and wise generation? I didn't feel so old or wise.

I thought of the story from the Talmud of Rabbi Meir and his wife Bruria. I imagined this wise and righteous rabbi going off to *shul* on a Sabbath morning. While he was gone, a terrible thing happened: their two sons suddenly died. He returned home and his wife, Bruria, had to tell her husband of the loss of their two beloved sons. She asked him what would be the right thing to do if someone entrusted her with precious jewels and then, after some time, asked for them back. Did she have to give them back? "Of course, you must return them," was the rabbi's reply. "They are not yours to keep." Then she showed him their sons.

My loved ones were like those precious jewels. They were not even gifts. Just on loan. For how long? Only God knew.

My intellect was comforted, but my heart still ached. It is said that we can only be partially comforted by others. Complete consolation for our losses can only come from God. There is a certain irony in all of this. We can cry and complain to God for our losses, and yet we can never recover from our grief without Him.

ANOTHER FUNERAL

People were surprised that we took Mom to Aunt Annette's funeral. The idea of her not going never entered our minds. It is true that she was fading in and out of reality, but she seemed to understand that her daughter had passed on. Even as her mind got more and more confused, I was seeing in Mom a strength of character that I hadn't noticed when I was younger.

There was a bit of confusion at the grave. In keeping with the observances of traditional Judaism, we believed that the grave had to be at least partially filled by family and friends before we left the gravesite. Before this was done, the rabbi who was performing the service instructed everyone to form two lines for the mourners to pass through as they left, in order to offer the traditional words of consolation. ("May God console you among the mourners of Zion and Jerusalem.")

My family and my sister's family decided that everyone else could leave if they chose to, but we would finish filling in the grave. Mom had been sitting on a portable chair. She refused to go. She would not budge. "I am not going until they are done!" was her comment. So everyone waited until we were done.

Mom sat in the living room most of the week and refused to go outside. When she asked, "Where's the box to sit on?" as *halacha* requires mourners to sit on lower than usual chairs, we told her that at her age she could sit on a regular chair. There were no crowds of people this time. Mom was often confused, but a part of her knew that her daughter had died. In her own way, in the quiet of the living room, she sat *shiva* this one last time.

CHAPTER SEVEN

SUMMER DECLINE

The summer came. The weather got warmer and sometimes we sat outside. Mom kept complaining because she liked to sit out front, but she said that she couldn't see past the bushes. Funny, I never really noticed it before. I always preferred to sit in the backyard and watch for rabbits and birds, but Mom was a city person. She preferred to sit in the front and watch the people and the cars go by. So we took the bushes out and extended the cement to make a bigger front porch. What else could I do? Every time we sat outside she would complain about the bushes, and each time we took a walk she would comment, "Look how nice that house looks. Just grass. No tall bushes."

Mom also had strong opinions about other things, like what kind of carrots I bought at the supermarket. She insisted that the best carrots were the ones with the green stems on top. She told me that they were worth the extra money. Mom always told me that quality was more important than quantity, whether it was food or clothing. I don't know what I would have done if I had a larger family, but I must admit that she was certainly right about those carrots!

One activity she persisted in doing on her own was making the string bean salad. It was a whole production. I fried the onions, cooked the string beans and boiled the eggs. Then she sat at the kitchen table and chopped everything by hand. Of course we had to buy a new chopper and wooden board because my utensils were not quite good enough. (I don't think she ever really forgave me for not bringing all of her dishes and utensils when she moved in.) Making the string bean salad became the end of each week ritual so that we could enjoy it for our Shabbat afternoon lunch.

As the summer passed, Mom became more confused. At first she made me write down the directions for the string bean salad so we wouldn't forget how to make it. Then she started to tell me that she just wasn't up to cooking. Soon after that she began to wander

around at night, which wasn't a problem until she started to fall. I decided to put an audio monitor in her room
so that I could hear her when she got up.

By August, her dementia had greatly increased.
She would cry out at night, sometimes for me but often
for people who were not present in the house—my
father, Annette and sometimes even for Andrew. Once
she started to walk out of the house and called to my
husband, "Good-bye, Mr. Bob." When he asked her
where she was going, she said, "to catch the subway to
Columbus Avenue."

Then she got very agitated. She would wander
around to the point of exhaustion. We couldn't get her
to sit down and rest. Bob followed her around to catch
her as she began to stumble and fall. She confused the
mirrored door with an elevator. She was trying to get in
to get to the ninth floor. She fell down again. Nobody
seemed to be able to calm her. I took her to the emergency room for an X-ray. For the first time, she didn't
know who I was. I cried to her doctor on the phone. He
asked, "What do you want to do? We'll do whatever
you want. Do you want to have her admitted?"

I didn't know what to do. Admit her and then
make steps toward a nursing home? I knew how much
she hated the idea of going to a nursing home. She had
complained to me so many times about how her sister
had ended up in a nursing home. This had been one of

her biggest fears. But she didn't even seem to know who I was. What else could I do?

Then I heard her voice calling me. "Sheila, Sheila," she called. A food tray had come and she was calling me to help her. That was my answer. I took her home.

But it didn't last long. She had another episode of agitation and not recognizing anyone. Again Bob followed her around in the hope that she wouldn't fall. Even her aide, Lorraine, had a hard time handling her. I looked at Lorraine and my husband as he followed her around. I knew that it was time. We had kept her home for as long as we could.

THE SEARCH FOR A HOME

It's not easy to get someone into a nursing home. Priority is given to people coming from the hospital. The doctor admitted her to the hospital and tried to find out why she was falling. I started making arrangements for a nursing home.

Mom had already been on Medicaid for a while, but they still wanted three years of her bank statements to prove that she never had more than $2,000 a month. Mom had kept most of her bank statements, but some of them were missing. I didn't know how long they would let her stay at the hospital, and I needed Medicaid approval before she could be accepted into a nursing facility. The people at the bank were nice enough to put a rush on sending us her records, and they even waived the usual fee because she really had very little money.

We began looking for a nursing home. I really wanted to find a Jewish environment. She had often complained about the lack of Jewishness in the home her sister had been in. The one Jewish home nearby would not accept her. They said they could not handle her dementia. She could have had a room in a non-Jewish home five minutes from my house. I went to see it. I felt like crying. This was so close by, but it was precisely the kind of home that Mom had always complained about.

The Hebrew Home for the Aged in Riverdale accepted her, but she would have to wait for a room. They didn't know how long this would take. Would the hospital wait? The home was over an hour away. How could I send her so far away?

My niece Wendy liked the idea. The Hebrew Home was about twenty minutes from my sister's house. She said that Mom had spent enough time with us, and it was only fair that she be closer to her. Maybe it was for the best. It was time to share in the responsibility. My family had been the caretakers for both fathers and my grandmother. I guess that it was time for a break.

In my usual codependent fashion, I was reluctant

to go away on the vacation we had planned with Mom still in the hospital. My sister encouraged us to go. She said that she would take care of things. Bob's associate, Karen, promised to visit her in the hospital. After all, how long could it possibly take for a room to open up?

We left for two weeks expecting Mom to be all settled in by the time we returned. To my horror, we found her still waiting in the hospital when we arrived home. It was a Friday in August. I was so angry. I started making phone calls and found out that there had been a room but they had given it to someone else because my grandmother's doctor was not available to sign her discharge papers and the covering doctor refused to sign because she was not his patient.

I felt the anger begin to boil. The Hebrew Home said there would be another room available on Monday but they would only hold it if I could guarantee her discharge from the hospital. My job was to convince the covering doctor to sign the necessary papers. I called him several times at his office. He would not accept or return any of my calls. I only had one hour left. The Hebrew Home needed a decision by 4:00 p.m. Then I decided to get tough. (Mom's strength had rubbed off on me after all.) I told the nurse that if the doctor did not get on the phone, I was going to come to his office and make a big scene until he would see me. He picked up the phone. I suppose by this time he was warned that I was pretty persistent. He finally agreed to do the discharge. Everything was arranged and Mom moved to the Hebrew Home on Monday.

A new pattern of life formed. September arrived. Ilana went back to school. Valerie went almost every day for the first few weeks to help get Mom settled in. Then she tried to go once a week and I tried for every other week. Mom seemed happy at the home. She wandered all over the unit. She ate well and was very friendly with some of the residents. When I went to visit I would take her to lunch in the restaurant on the premises. For a while, life was calm.

CHAPTER EIGHT

PROBLEMS BEGIN

THE TEETH

I took the elevator to the sixth floor and found Mom in the common area, like usual. I noticed that her top false teeth were missing. The conversation went like this:

"Mom, you are missing your top teeth."

"I know."

"Where are they?"

"I threw them out."

"Mom, why would you throw out your teeth?"

"They were dirty."

"If they were dirty, we could have cleaned them. You need your teeth. How are you going to eat?"

"How much do I eat?"

With that, Mom started to laugh. I think that she was impressed with herself at how clever she was. I had to laugh with her.

So they searched the Home but without success. The teeth were nowhere to be found. I felt so bad because I know how proud she had been of those teeth. She had often told me that they were excellent teeth and the dentist had given her a break and only charged her two thousand dollars for them even though they were worth much more. But now, they seemed unimportant to her.

The social worker made her an appointment with the dentist to have new teeth made. We went to lunch one day and she managed to eat a hamburger with just the bottoms. Weeks passed and I still hadn't heard anything about her teeth. On one of my visits, I asked the nurse when she would be getting her new teeth. I was told, "She went to the dentist but did not cooperate. The dentist said that she will not see her again unless she is accompanied by a family member." I felt my anger begin to build. Why didn't they call me? I would have gone with her weeks before. I checked my anger and made another appointment for the following week.

As soon as I saw Mom she told me how happy she was to see me.

"I'm so glad to see you. You know I need to see a dentist."

"I know. That's why I am here. We will go together."

"Today? What time?"

"11:15."

"Well we better get going."

Now understand that it was only 10:50 and we only had to go down to the main floor. But Mom is always in a rush to go even when there is no place to go. So we left immediately and got there fifteen minutes early. Then she got anxious and wanted to leave.

"Let's go. There's no point in waiting here."

"Mom, we are waiting for the dentist. I think we should stay."

"Well, what's taking so long?"

"Your appointment isn't for another ten minutes, and there is someone ahead of us."

"Let's go."

"We need to wait a little longer. You need to see the dentist."

The conversation continued like this for the remaining ten minutes. When we finally got to see the dentist, I understood the problem.

"I can't work with your grandmother if she doesn't cooperate."

"That's why I'm here."

"Sometimes old people can't tolerate their teeth anymore. That's why they take them out all of the time and lose them."

"Well, she had been wearing her teeth successfully until they got lost."

"It's a degenerative problem."

I felt like saying, "Did you ever talk to my grandmother? Do you still consider her to be a person?" Did you explain to her how important it is for her to cooperate so that she can get a new set of teeth? Or did you just write her off as another one of those old, demented seniors, who are too hopeless to try to help?" But I kept quiet. The fitting took no more than five minutes.

I went back two more times for these five-minute fittings, doubting that any of this would ever work. The teeth did not seem to be comfortable for Mom, and the dentist was convinced that it was due to Mom's condition.

Finally the teeth were ready and I made another trip to the Home so that I could go with Mom to the dentist once again. This time, I arrived on her floor and noticed that there were no teeth in her mouth.

"Mom, where are your teeth? Did you throw them away?"

"No. It was the other ones I threw away."

"So where are the bottoms?"

"I don't know."

She started to laugh. How much does she need to eat anyway?

I said, "Mom, you're like the angels? You don't need any food?"

She liked that idea.

The nurses said that she was managing to eat her regular diet, even without any teeth. She looked thin to me but they said that she hadn't lost any weight. Again, what could I say? We picked up the new top teeth, even though she never wore them. I found an extra set of bottoms in my house and brought them. I knew she wouldn't wear them either.

THE FALL

It was a Tuesday and I was working on this book. The phone rang. It was the social worker from the nursing home. Mom had fallen and her glasses had cut her nose. Bob just happened to be free that day, so we went together to see her. I was expecting to find her in bed and unable to go down for our usual lunch, so we stopped to eat before we went up to her floor. We found her sitting in the common area and as soon as we saw her she said, "Let's go." So we went to the restaurant and ordered dessert, while she tried, toothless, to manage a turkey sandwich.

"I'm so frightened. You know I fell down. Maybe you could stay with me at the house tonight?" she asked me.

"I'm sorry, I won't be able to stay. I will have to go home. But the nurses are here. Please ask them for help if you need it." I tried to convince her.

She talked a lot about the fall. Some of it I understood and some of it I didn't. That's the way our conversations seemed to be going. Part clear and part unrecognizable. But I was happy that she talked through her thoughts and problems even though I didn't always know what she was talking about.

LUNCH AT THE RIVERVIEW CAFE

The Riverview Cafe is the name of the restaurant at the Hebrew Home for the Aged. It is a wonderful place. The prices are reasonable like a cafeteria, but there is table service so it is more like being at a cozy restaurant. There is a big window with a beautiful view of the Hudson River.

The only problem is that when you go there with Mom you have to eat quickly. As soon as she is done eating she is ready to go. When Bob came with me one day I warned him.

"Eat quick. You won't have much time."

True to form, Mom finished before us and was ready to go.

"Okay, let's go," Mom ordered.

"I didn't finish my lunch yet," I replied.

"I can't sit here anymore," Mom simply stated.

"How about a cup of coffee?" I asked.

The coffee gave me enough time to finish my lunch but Bob wanted to order dessert! Mom and I left him to finish his dessert by himself. She couldn't wait any longer. But where would we go? I tried to walk around and look at some jewelry that someone was selling on tables in the hall, but she was not interested.

"Where are you taking me? I have to get out of here," Mom exclaimed.

So we took her back upstairs to the common area. This is where she seemed to be able to sit for a while. She cried a bit.

"What kind of life is this? Just look at those people. How will I get home to my children to take care of them? They need me," she stated sadly.

I tried to comfort her. I held her hand and listened. What do you say to a person whose entire life had disappeared? Her husband, sisters, brothers, children and friends were gone. Even a part of herself, her ability to think, cook and do things for others, was gone. I felt so useless and ineffective. How could I possibly help her when all the pieces of her life were missing?

She was so tired. We helped her into bed. I told her that I would be leaving but that I would be back.

"How will I find you," she worriedly asked.

"Don't worry. I'll find you," I answered.

ANOTHER FALL

All of the demands of life were pulling at me. What should I do first? This particular morning I was going to teach a class. I usually studied with Dr. Blema Feinstein on Tuesday mornings but sometimes I would skip the class and go to see Mom. But Blema could not make the class and asked me to teach it. It was a week before Passover. Chances are there would not be many people there. If I wasn't teaching it, I probably would have skipped it and gone to the nursing home. Well, I figured, I'd go to see Mom on Wednesday instead.

There were only two of us. We learned together for about an hour. I left the cell phone in the car. What could be so important that it couldn't wait for an hour? I checked the phone. There were four increasingly frantic calls from my husband. Mom had fallen again. This time she broke her hip. She was on the way to a hospital in the city at that very moment.

A wave of codependent guilt hit me. Maybe if I had been there this wouldn't have happened. I could have prevented her fall. If I had been there she would have been walking with me instead of walking alone.

I felt short of breath and felt a pain in the pit of my stomach. Bob was telling me something, but I wasn't focusing on what he was saying. Try to listen, I said to myself. What is he saying?

"Listen, you couldn't have helped her. She fell at three o'clock in the morning. There is nothing you could have done."

I thought that I had overcome my codependent feelings of responsibility for everyone. I thought that I had finally realized that only God is in control of the world and not me. But there it was again. I had automatically felt responsible. I guess that's why we say that we are recovering codependents instead of cured.

I felt compelled to rush into Manhattan to the hospital. I sat for a few minutes to compose myself. It was twelve o'clock in the afternoon. I knew that I had to also take care of myself. That compulsion was just another manifestation of my codependent nature. I stopped for something to eat. I called my sister. I wouldn't try to handle this by myself. An hour later, I left for the city.

Poor Mom, she was so frightened and confused. They were trying to keep her in a lying down position, but she only wanted to get up and walk. My sister came and her husband came in the evening. My codependent part wanted to stay all night in the hospital. But I took an honest look at myself. I was totally exhausted. Passover was coming, and my husband was swamped with tax season work. I needed to go home. So we hired aides to stay with my grandmother in the hospital, and I went home. My sister and I took turns visiting in the city, but we made sure that she always had an aide by her side.

After a few days at the hospital Mom was back to the Hebrew Home. At first, she did amazingly well. I went to see her at the Home after Passover. She improved physically but she had become so confused. I was lucky to understand two or three of the words that she spoke. Most of her talking was incoherent. And yet, she was able to communicate to me exactly what she needed. She let me know when she wanted to walk and when she had enough. When lunch arrived, she was very firm about which part of it she wanted to eat and which part she refused. She looked so bedraggled and forlorn, I tried to convince her to get her hair done. I even got her as far as the beautician's chair. But no. There was no way that she was going to stay in that chair. She flashed an angry countenance at me and let me know in no uncertain terms that she was getting up.

Who was this demented grandmother that sat before me? I realized that I barely knew her. You go and visit grandparents and they feed you and give you sweets. You play a game or watch the television with your sister while your parents talk to your grandparent. Later, when I was older, I would visit her myself. We went for walks and of course, again we ate together. Short visits, and then I was on my way. I don't think I ever really knew her as a person besides just being my grandmother.

But now I sensed a strength in Mom that I had never paid attention to before. She had the ability that I had been lacking, to stand firm. Perhaps this is what had kept her going so many years when so many other mothers seemed to have passed away at a young age. Was it possible that here in my grandmother was that model of a balance between kindness and strength or restraint that I had been seeking?

I had seen the kindness. She had been there for her children and grandchildren. Making food and knitting afghans for everyone. Helping my sister pack when she moved. My great-grandmother had lived with Mom when my father was young. I know that my father hadn't been too healthy as a child and that Mom took care of him. Both my father and aunt had suffered from depression. This had to have been difficult for her as their mother. She also took care of my grandfather who was sick for many years with a terrible case of arthritis and then managed on her own all those years after he died. She cooked food for sick neighbors, even when she was close to ninety and was unable to see too well anymore. But she survived, through all the hardships, all the illnesses and all the deaths. How did she do it? Perhaps she knew when to give and when to hold back. I now saw a woman who had given to others but also knew how to stand up for herself.

And then I remembered the stories of my great-grandmother, Ida. She was a strong woman also. She divorced a bad husband in the years when almost no one divorced their husband. She remarried but when her sons moved to Warsaw and her husband hesitated to move, she told him, "I am going to Warsaw with my children. You can come or stay, as you please." Later, the three older brothers went to America. Her husband died and she was left with three young girls to support. Eventually she made it to the United States with her three daughters, and reunited with her three sons. Ida had been a seamstress. She was so talented that she could sew a dress just from seeing it in a store window, without a pattern. Everyone told me that I got her "*goldena hent*" (golden hands). I also hope that somewhere inside I got her *gevura* — her sense of strength.

A VISIT

Most of the time I went to visit Mom by myself. Occasionally either Bob or Ilana joined me. One week, I was feeling particularly tired. Bob offered to go with me. He was so busy with work that I almost told him that I would go by myself. If I hadn't been feeling so tired, I probably would have told him to stay home and finish his work. But I thought about it. He needed to go, too. We all needed to take a break from our busy lives from time to time to do a reality check.

If we get so busy with our "work," it is easy to lose sight of what is truly important. King David tells us in Psalms, "Man is like a breath, his days are like a passing shadow." We all know those words, but we rarely live with the significance of this truth. We tend to act as if we will live forever and everything that we do is of utmost importance. I sometimes wonder, how important is all of my busy activity? Spending time with old people, especially those with dementia, sends me right back to the real world, the world where people get old and sick and where nobody lives forever.

I spend a lot of time with old people, both in my family and at work. Somehow, if a person is physically incapacitated but maintains cognitive function, it is easier to see how life could still be purposeful. Their achievements can be measured. But is the purpose of life to accumulate achievements? What can the person who has lost clarity of thought achieve? Does a person need to produce something substantial in order to justify their existence? Maybe it is enough just to exist and leave the purpose in God's hands.

Mom was moved to a unit for residents with severe dementia. I was a little shocked when I saw Mom this time, so I was so glad that Bob had come along. Physically she had lost more weight. She looked so thin and frail that I was frightened. The social worker had warned me that she was hardly eating. She would only eat some fruit and drink some food supplements. The entire staff was trying so hard. The dietitian sat with her at every meal. They kept trying different kinds of food. They took her out of a wheelchair and put her into a regular chair, so she would be more comfortable at the table. I was continuously amazed and grateful at how attentive and supportive the staff was at the Hebrew Home. While we were there, the social worker, head nurse, dietitian and recreation therapist all came over to see how she was doing.

The aide brought her lunch. With my help, Mom ate quite a bit of her food including the chicken and the carrots. I got that codependent urge to take care of Mom myself. Maybe I should ride up each day to make sure she eats at least one meal? But I checked myself. Mom's life was not in my hands, but in God's hands. As she got to know the staff better, perhaps she would let them help her more with the food. Even if I came every day, it did not mean that she would eat just because I was there. Her eating would also be her choice.

It seemed like Mom had been slowly disconnecting from life, letting go perhaps. First she threw away her teeth. Then she stopped wearing her glasses. She refused to go to the beauty parlor for a wash and cut. During the most recent visit I noticed that she no longer asked to go to the bathroom, and that she had lost her interest in eating. She talked very little to us and her face seemed to betray almost no emotion. She smiled just a few times. Mostly her expression was blank.

I remember thinking, "Where are you Mom? Are you still there, only hidden deeply away? Have you already left us behind in this world of suffering and pain? Are you in a better place?"

THE PICTURE

Each door in Mom's unit had a place to hang photographs of the person who resided in each particular room. I looked around at all of the pictures. Many of them listed the person's profession. Neurologist. Bookkeeper. Secretary. Prizefighter. Homemaker. Sheet metal worker. Piano player. What struck me was the fact that it didn't really matter what they had done. They were all here together. Here, they were all equal.

I took a picture of Mom and Pop to an office supply store to copy for her door. The picture frame was glued together. The woman at the store helped me to pry it open. It took a long time. She made a copy on their color copier, which also took a bit longer. She gave me one copy and then went to make another one.

While I waited, I gazed at the picture for a while. I felt the tears welling up in my eyes. Mom and Pop weren't much older than I am now. Mom looked so young and beautiful. What happened to all of those years? I thought about the way she was now. When I looked into her eyes I thought, "Will this be me?"

My emotions got all mixed up. Who was I crying for? As Mom faded away, I felt that I was losing my connection with all of the older generation of my family. I was crying for Mom but I was also crying for my mother, father, Aunt Shirley, and Aunt Annette. Was I also crying for myself? I think so. I think I was crying for my childhood. For the fact that there was no one left to take care of me. For the fact that I too would grow old and pass away.

ONE WEEK LATER

"Hello, Sheila."

Was I hearing correctly? She hadn't called me by my name for a long time. I often felt that there was a recognition, that I was a known and friendly face. But on this visit, she greeted me by name as soon as she saw me walk into the room.

I usually visited Mom every other week. Each visit was an exhausting one. Two hours in traffic, an emotionally draining two-hour visit and then returning home again with traffic for another two-hour ride. This time, I went after just a week, because Mom seemed so frail and forlorn on the previous visit. I thought perhaps if I came again, then at least she would eat again.

The woman who greeted me was still thin and frail but she was also hopeful and cheerful. Just as we were beginning to have a conversation, the nurse told me that a care plan meeting was taking place and that the team wanted to talk to me. I told Mom that I needed to go and talk to her doctors, and that I would be right back.

"Your grandmother is still not eating very much," the dietitian informed me.

"I just saw her. She looks so much better than last week. She even called me by my name."

"Yes. In other ways she is doing quite well."

"How much does she weigh?"

"Eighty-seven pounds."

"But she eats sometimes?"

"Yes, she eats sometimes. But she is not eating enough to maintain her weight. Do you know how she would feel about a feeding tube?"

I felt like I had been hit with a ton of bricks. I had

just seen her. For that moment I was filled with optimism. She had seemed cheerful and happy. How could they be telling me this now?

"I think that she would hate the idea of a feeding tube!"

"Well think about it. It isn't necessary right now, but if she continues to refuse to eat, it'll just be a matter of time before she will get sick."

"I'll think about it and also talk to my sister. I'll let you know."

What else could I say? I knew that all of those people at that meeting had been trying really hard to get Mom to eat. They offered her food in different locations and at different times. The dietitian had sat with her and tried her best to coax her to eat. But a food tube?

I returned to the room where my grandmother was sitting. She seemed so full of spirit. I hadn't planned on taking her to the restaurant for lunch but I thought that perhaps it was worth a try.

"You want to go downstairs for lunch today?" I asked tentatively.

"Why not!" she cheerfully replied.

Walking down to the restaurant was a long process. We stopped at almost every chair we passed so that Mom could rest. After a five-minute rest, she was off again. She greeted everyone that passed by with a cheerful wave and a friendly hello.

I couldn't believe how much she ate. An entire half of a chicken salad sandwich and a bowl of mushroom barley soup. She ate more than I did!

Then it was the long trek back. Again we stopped to rest. As we approached the elevator, she was tired again. We went into a nearby lounge so that she could sit and rest. There happened to be a piano in the room. I thought, "Should I try?" Each time I had tried before to play for her, she was not able to sit very long. Part of her dementia was this drive she has to keep getting up and walking. But this day had gone so well. What did I have to lose?

I helped her into a chair and then pulled it right up next to the piano. I played and I sang to her. She stayed and listened. She smiled and she was relaxed. I made a mental resolution to practice some Yiddish songs as well as some classical songs for my next visit.

The dietitian came into the room. I explained to her that I used to play for her and this is also what I do since I work as a recreation/music therapist in a nursing home.

"A little one-on-one," she said.

"Yes," I answered. "A little one-on-one."

We went back upstairs to her floor. I stayed for a few more minutes, and then I had to start my long trek home. Even though I felt good about the visit, a cloud seemed to find its way and settle over me in the car. A feeding tube. They wanted me to think about a feeding tube. Was my initial response the right one? Didn't she have the right to decide if she wanted to eat or not? Maybe she did, but maybe she didn't. I suddenly realized that this was really a question for a rabbi.

I spoke with two rabbis. They concurred. She did not have the right to decide not to eat. Every moment of life is precious, and we have an obligation to assist a person to live as long as possible. She had too much dementia to really make a conscious decision about this issue. To withhold a feeding tube would be tantamount to an assisted suicide.

I spoke with my sister. Her initial response was similar to mine. She would not have wanted a feeding tube, but then she added something else. "Do we really want to prolong her life the way it is now?"

How would I tell her that I had learned the lesson of strength of character from Mom, even as she faded in and out of the reality that surrounded her? Did Valerie also see how Mom touched others and brought forth a response of kindness and compassion from her caretakers and that it was not up to us to decide life's value?

Did I dare to say that even if we couldn't see any benefit or purpose to Mom's life, it was only because our vision was too narrow? The only fact we had to rely on was that if someone was alive, that was God's plan. He knew the purpose even if we couldn't see it.

I decided on a more down-to-earth response. I told

her that to starve to death was a terrible death. And she was not unhappy or suffering. We watched Daddy starve to death. I would not want to see Mom have to go through this. I would talk to her doctor to find out what signs would indicate that her life was in danger. I wanted her to be able to rely on food for as long as possible. I did not want them to consider a feeding tube because it might be easier for them than continuing to coax her into eating. I wanted them to try everything else first. But I did not want her to starve to death.

I hung up the phone and I felt the awesome weight of making decisions that involved someone else's life. I also felt somewhat reassured. I did not have to decide based on my own thoughts and ideas. Jewish law was there to lead me to the correct decision. I took a few breaths and relaxed. Whatever would be, would be in God's hands, not mine. Not bad for a recovering codependent!

CHAPTER NINE

THREE
STRIKES

W hy is it that just when you think you have everything figured out, a curve ball is sent in your direction? I had decided in my mind that we would agree to the feeding tube only when Mom actually got too weak to eat. Why rush it? Maybe she would start to eat more again anyway. I made a note to talk to the doctor to determine at what point her life would be in danger.

I spoke to a few nurses that I knew, trying to educate myself about this possibility. One suggested that if she must have a feeding tube, bolus feeding would be better. There seemed to be two ways to administer a feeding tube. There was a tendency to connect the patient to a pump at night, which worked for about six hours while the person was asleep in bed. The nurse I spoke to felt this was not the best way. She found the patients who were fed this way were lethargic during the daytime hours when they were not receiving any nutrients. Bolus feeding was administered by a syringe for about twenty minutes at regular meal times. This more closely approximated normal food intake, and she felt that patients responded with much more energy this way.

Fortified by my information and resolve, I approached the nurse and the social worker at the Hebrew Home. That is when I felt that I struck out. First, they told me that we could not wait until Mom was too weak to eat, because that would mean that she would also be too weak to survive the procedure, which, by the way, required an overnight stay in the hospital. Second, the social worker informed me that when dementia residents stop eating, they do not start again. The disease along with its behavior is progressive. Third, the nurse told me that they did not do bolus feeding at the Hebrew Home.

So I continued my investigation. I talked to everyone I knew about feeding tubes to see if anyone else had any knowledge or experience. My sister spoke to someone whose mother had found it very painful and uncomfortable. I spoke to someone else whose mother would beg her to take out the tube because of the discomfort. Finally, they took it out. Her mother died two months later, not from starvation—she actually tried to eat again—but because she had been so weakened by the two procedures, of putting in the tube and then taking it out.

I had learned that, while we may never do anything to shorten anyone's life, we are also not required to prolong someone's death, especially if the patient is in terrible pain. If we can control the pain with drugs, then we should attempt to prolong an individual's life. In the final stages, when death is imminent, no intervention should be made. According to the opinion of Rabbi Moshe Feinstein (a widely accepted Torah authority), pain seemed to be the critical element. It is important to note that this includes both mental and physical suffering. In Rabbi Feinstein's words, "If the patient is not suffering any pain—in other words, if there is no burden in his maintaining his present state— there is no reason why he should not be given all medical care to prolong his life as much as possible."

Being deprived of either oxygen or food causes pain, while providing someone with oxygen and/or food does not fall into the category of prolonging life, but of making a person more comfortable. Any deliberate hastening of death of even a terminally ill patient is prohibited as murder. Active euthanasia is not allowed in Judaism. But if the patient is dying from an incurable illness and all therapy has failed or is not available, the physician's role changes from that of a curer to that of a carer. Only supportive care is required at that stage, such as food and water, good nursing care and maximal psychosocial support.

Mom's own situation did not seem clear because she was eating, just not enough to maintain her weight. Difficult decisions are just that—very difficult.

I went to see Mom the next week. This time she did not greet me by name, but she still seemed happy to see me. Again, we went down to the restaurant and she ate everything that we ordered. We sat down to rest on the way back to her unit. I did not know how much she could understand, but I felt that I had to try to convince her to keep eating.

"Mom," I said, "You have to eat. And not just with me or Valerie. All the time. You have lost a lot of weight. They want to put you on a feeding tube. You will hate that. You will have to go back to the hospital. Please, please, just eat."

I don't know how many times I repeated this message. I gave her a little massage and then I would repeat the message. Each day after this, I kept praying to God that she should start to eat again. Not such a big miracle! Just let her eat.

My sister went to see her the following week. She spoke to the dietitian.

"How is she doing?" my sister asked.

"Well, she is eating a little more—not a lot. But she is feeding herself as soon as she gets her food, even though she eats a small amount."

"And her weight?"

"It's not a lot, but she did gain one pound."

"We were hoping that she would maintain her weight. Even a gain of one pound is terrific!"

Mom was a survivor. I didn't know what had gotten through to her. The nurses and dietician who worked relentlessly to get her to eat? Did she understand what I had told her? Did she just feel hungry again? Did God guide her to eat?

I did not know how long this would last. At this point, I felt that we would let them put in the feeding tube if she could not maintain her weight by eating and the feeding tube would help her. What I did know was that nothing is absolute except for God. There is always hope.

ANOTHER WEEK, ANOTHER POUND

A week later, I was back at the Hebrew Home. "This is my granddaughter," Mom said to the woman who sat next to her. I don't even know if that woman knew what a granddaughter was. She spoke only

Spanish.

A few times Mom would start a thought and leave it hanging. I tried to fill in the blanks.

"I don't eat," Mom informed me.

"You need to eat. If you don't eat they will put in a feeding tube. You would hate that. You have to keep eating."

"They bring me food in the morning."

"And do you eat breakfast?"

No reply.

"If you have your health…," Mom began.

"If you have your health, life is wonderful," I continued.

"If not…," Mom began again.

"Then life is not so wonderful," I concluded.

Some of her thoughts were with me and some were elsewhere.

"Melvin always comes home late," she told me.

What could I reply about my father, her son, who had passed away over a year ago? This time, I just listened.

We had a very productive visit. We walked for about an hour and then went to the restaurant to eat. Bob had come along on this visit and still could not believe how quickly lunch passed with Mom. She ate quickly and then was ready to go again. She was still walking until she could barely stand up.

Again we stopped at all of the chairs to rest. Again I played three songs for her on the piano. This time I brought my book of Yiddish songs. All of the residents in the lounge wanted me to continue. "Play another one. Don't stop now!" But Mom was up and ready to go. "I have to go with Grandma," I said. "But I promise to come back again another day to play some more."

We went back upstairs and this time Mom really surprised me. Her hair had gotten pretty long. It had been many months since she had sat still and let the beautician give her a haircut. I talked about how we used to go to the beautician together.

"Remember how we used to go get our hair cut together?"

"Yes."

"You always liked it nice and short like mine."

"Short. Yes."

"Would you like me to check and see if the beautician is in? Maybe you could get a nice short haircut for the summer."

"Yes. A short haircut."

The beautician was in, and available with no other customers at the moment. I walked back and found that Mom had fallen asleep. I hated to wake her so I waited. After about five minutes, her eyes opened. I saw my opportunity.

"The beautician is in. Shall we go for a haircut?"

"Yes."

So slowly we walked to the beautician's room. Luckily Bob was there because Mom was still half asleep, and he supported her other side. When the beautician tried to wash her hair I could see that she was frightened. I suggested that we skip the wash and move right to the haircut. Her hair was very clean. They must have washed it in the shower. She sat Mom back up and sprayed her hair to make it wet. As she started to cut, I saw Mom relax. I told the beautician that she didn't have too much time. Mom never sat too long in one spot. But this time, I didn't have to worry. Mom was so relaxed that she fell asleep.

So the beautician cut her hair, blew it dry and even curled it with a curling iron. I told Mom how beautiful she looked. She smiled. I kissed her hands and then she laughed and she kissed my hands.

We walked back to the hallway by the nurses' station. Mom was very relaxed and peaceful. Again she spoke Yiddish to the woman next to her who answered her in Spanish. Neither woman seemed to notice that the other was speaking a different language. Two other women were sitting on the other side of Mom. They were whispering and giggling like two school girls. One had her arm around the other. In a different time and place, the difference in the color of their skin might have kept them apart. Here, they also did not seem to notice any differences or care.

We heard a nurse coaxing someone to eat in the dining room. "Bessie, don't you want to eat just a little bit?"

I said to all of the ladies, "Isn't it funny how hard we try to lose weight all of our lives and here they are always trying to get everyone to eat?"

"They are always telling us to eat," one woman replied.

Then everyone laughed. But I guess that the coaxing sometimes worked. The good news: Mom was now up to eighty-nine pounds. She was doing better than maintaining her weight. She was gaining. So for now, the crisis about the feeding tube was over. As long as she kept eating and maintaining her weight, she would be okay.

"We have to go now," I told Mom.

"If you have to go, then go," she replied very matter of factly.

"I'll be back soon," I promised.

Bob and I stood across from them as we waited for the elevator.

"Such nice people," one lady announced to no one in particular as she pointed to us.

"Thank you," I replied.

The elevator door opened and we waved goodbye. All of the ladies waved back to us. A good visit. How long would she last? Did we ever know the answer to that question?

CHAPTER TEN

TIME
to THINK

❧

The crisis seemed to be behind us for now. Mom kept gaining about a pound each week. Everyone at the Home was thrilled. She had defied the odds. They had painted a bleak picture. Once a person with dementia stopped eating, they never returned to eating. The disease was progressive. But Mom was the exception. She was eating again.

Life fell into a routine. I continued to visit every week or two, worked at the Veterans Home and tried to maintain my family and home. Something new crept into my schedule—free time. Life was calm and filled with small spaces of unscheduled time. With this time I began to read more and to investigate my latest passion—the soul and what happens to it after our bodies cease to exist. I suppose I was trying to grapple with the loss of so many people I loved.

What I discovered encouraged me and strengthened my sad heart. According to such philosophical giants as Maimonides, the soul may have a variety of functions, but each of us has one indivisible soul that sustains, develops and motivates our physical bodies. Our soul gives us the ability to do everything, from using our senses to thinking and distinguishing between good and bad. All souls were created before even the first man. Each soul is unique and serves as a blueprint for the body that it will join.

In my readings, it said that the soul is first reluctant to enter the body and then reluctant to leave. This would certainly explain our attachment to life and our fear of death. Every existence that God creates is a good one. Why would we want to leave? But if we must leave, at least we can find solace in the knowledge that the next life will be even better than the last. Our existence in the next world is described as "a bliss beyond which there is nothing more blissful" in "a world unending." This physical life should be cherished not only for the pleasures that we have in this world, but also because it is through our actions in this world that we can attain the great good in store for us in the World to Come. All of the joy and pleasure to be found in even the longest of lives on earth cannot come close to the spiritual satisfaction of one moment in the World to Come.

THE PURPOSE OF LIFE

I recalled a recent conversation I had with a family member. I was thinking about Mom and how hard it was to get to see her. I had always hoped that she would be able to live with us and avoid the nursing home scene.

"I have such mixed feelings about Mom," I began.

"I don't. She had a good life."

"It's true, she did pretty well for the first ninety years. And the Hebrew Home for the Aged is a wonderful place, even if it is a nursing home."

"Besides, often she doesn't even know who you are when you go to visit her."

"She always knows me," I insisted.

"Really the only question I have is why she still goes on. A life like that doesn't really have any purpose."

A life like that doesn't have a purpose. How many times had I heard that before? From my father when he talked about his life after my mother died. From the residents I work with at the Long Island State Veterans Home.

And now I was hearing it about Mom. No purpose?

So then what is the purpose of life anyway? Is it just to produce as many material goods as possible? *The Path of the Just* tells us that the purpose of life is to attach oneself to God. For me, attaching myself to God means that I try to get as physically and mentally healthy as possible so that I can become the type of person God intended human beings to be. To grow spiritually and make morally correct choices.

So who is serving the higher purpose in existence?

By taking care of my father, then Harry and then Mom, we were certainly helping them. We gave my father a place in our home to get stronger, so that he could eventually return to his home. Later, we helped him so that he could stay in his home right up until a month before he passed away. We also gave Harry a home with us so that he could be closer to all of his children. Instead of remaining in Florida, and waiting for an occasional visit from one of his children, he was close enough for them to visit him as often as they wanted. He was able to spend his last seven months going to dinner and movies with his children, visiting with his grandchildren and doing whatever he wanted, whenever he wanted.

And what about Mom? She was so frightened when she first came to live with us because she thought that people were breaking into her apartment. She was also terrified of ending up in a nursing home. We provided her with a safe place and supported her when she had to face the death of both of her children. Then we found her such a wonderful nursing home that she didn't even think it was a nursing home. She thought that she was in an apartment in the Bronx.

Very high purposes, indeed.

What did we get in return? Certainly not material rewards. So they had no purpose?

Certainly they had a purpose — a very high purpose. In fact, they gave us a lot more than we gave to them. In general, Bob and I took on our fathers as our project. We were united in trying to provide them the best possible care and making their last months as comfortable and happy as we could. We were a team with an assignment. And we worked so well with each other that our love for each other became refreshed and renewed. We were also left with fresh memories of special times, fun activities and quiet moments of closeness with the people that we loved.

In the process I was personally challenged to overcome my codependent personality, and I finally learned how to take care of others while still looking after myself. I am happier now and more content with my life than I have been for a long time. So I dislike hearing people say that the old and sick serve no purpose. The extreme example of this philosophy were the Nazis who felt justified in ridding the world of "useless" people.

I work with the elderly. They often give me a lot more than I could ever give them. After working at the Vets Home for more than three years, for the first time I was reassigned to carry out programs with the Adult Day Care. I felt very nervous and unsure of myself. These would all be new people. I had been doing music therapy mostly with low functioning, medically fragile residents. This would be a whole new experience.

On my first day I was assigned to work with another music therapist who had been involved in this program for about a year. Since this was the beginning of January, we were going to use hand bells with the song "Auld Lang Syne." This was great. I hadn't used the bells and I had always wanted to, as they were not appropriate for the residents that I had been working with until now. This would also give me a chance to feel out the situation and get to know some of the people without having to be in charge.

I arrived at work feeling pretty optimistic, and as I walked in the door, I heard the news. The other music therapist had called in sick. The art therapist would work with me in the morning, and I would be on my own in the afternoon. So much for my gradual intro-duction.

After the morning I had an hour to eat lunch and decide what to do in the afternoon. Do I still try to do the bells? Nothing was arranged or organized. I could take the easy way out and either play music bingo with them or just do a general sing-along. Do I take a chance and go in with a splash or do I play it safe?

I guess I was feeling adventuresome. So I brought the bells, but took along all of my music for a sing-along—a back-up plan just in case the bells failed.

There was one woman who I noticed in the morning. She had been wearing her gloves all day. Was she cold? I doubt it since they keep the heat very high in the Home. Was she spending the day waiting to go home? I didn't know for sure. When I first offered her a bell, she declined. She would just watch.

After watching for a while, she decided to take a bell and join in. Then, an amazing thing happened. She took off her gloves and reached into her bag to pull out a New Years hat to wear. Her comments?

"I can't believe that I'm learning to play music at this age! I'm having more fun than I had in my whole life!"

"How old are you?" I gently asked.

"Ninety-six."

Then, after a very successful rendition of "Auld Lang Syne" on the bells, I began to play the piano for a sing-along. Not only did she sing, but she took the microphone and led a few of the songs. Then she asked me:

"When are you coming back?"

"Not for three weeks."

"Oh, I don't know if I will live that long!"

"You better, because I'll be looking for you."

"You're collecting the bells? I wanted to take them to practice and show my daughter."

I had walked into the session feeling anxious and nervous. I walked out feeling happy and confident. Does that old woman's life serve a purpose? She improved my self-esteem more than any psychiatrist could. So whose life has a higher purpose anyway?

And what about inspiration? If someone inspires someone else, does that person have a purpose? I remember the elder law attorney telling my father how he inspired him by his courage and his concern for his children. Why didn't my father ever see the value in that? Every day I go to work I am inspired by the veterans. Most of them were in World War II. Most of them are now in wheelchairs. Some have limbs that either don't function properly or are missing. Some can't speak. Some can't think clearly. Yet, so many of them give me a smile or a warm hello when they see me. They still support and help each other, as if they were still on active duty with the army. The one who can walk pushes another in a wheelchair. The younger veteran helps the older one find the correct unit when he gets confused. A resident who can get to a program by himself tells me about someone else on his floor who needs help. A younger male resident befriends one of the few female older residents and convinces her to start coming to recreation programs. The stories go on and on. People interacting, helping each other, inspiring each other to feel a little bit better.

Every life has a purpose. No one has the right to judge if one life is more valuable than another. We each need to grow and help each other to grow. We all have the ability to improve our lives and the lives of others. Our purpose is not to serve ourselves by making more money or producing more material goods. Our purpose is to serve God and do His Will.

Of course, there is a price to be paid. We get close to others and then they are gone.

I'm a better person for all the people who have touched my life. But life is a paradox. I'm healthier and more satisfied with what I have. I feel more love for my family and joy in my heart. But that very heart has missing pieces. It grows with each connection and then a piece breaks off with each loss.

Not long after my mother passed away, I was cooking and I burned myself. It was very painful and all I could think was, "I need my Mommy." This intense feeling of loss happens to me from time to time, and then I remind myself of what it says in *Ethics of the Fathers.* God is all knowing, all powerful and all good and this world was always meant to be temporary, like a corridor to the World to Come.

We can hide our old people in nursing facilities and pretend that life goes on forever. But sooner or later, it will be us who are getting older. Then where will we go? Where will we hide?

I will cherish the memories of those I loved who are no longer here. I will continue to seek inspiration from those who are around me. And when the losses hurt too much, I will try to remember that God is in charge, and not me. He has a plan for the world and it has to be a good one. I pray for His help and direction and try to find joy in the very present moments of my life.

There was a recent article in the newspaper examining why so many current movies deal with death. After listing the movies and their individual themes and ideas, the article concluded that these movies are well attended, not because people want to learn more about death but because people want to know more about how to live.

There is a teaching that it is better to spend time in a house of mourning than in a house of joy. It is in the house of mourning where one will learn best how to live. Karen, Bob's associate at the time, told me that her attitude about relationships changed as a result of having to deal with sickness and death. After attending the funeral of a friend's husband and spending a day with another friend who may have a life-threatening, inoperable condition in her brain, Karen told me that she decided to stop arguing with her sister or her husband about small, petty differences. Being in contact with death helps us to set our priorities straight, to value and cherish the moments of peace and contentment in our day.

We can hide from old people. We can distance ourselves from sickness and death. But then where will we go to learn how to live? How will we learn that life is temporary and that we must be grateful for every day? Who will teach us to treasure each moment? How will we come to understand that each of us has enormous value and serve a purpose for as long as we are alive? When will we be able to see that the most important reasons for our existence are spiritual accomplishments and not material production?

Taking care of older people has also helped me to come to terms with the codependent flaws in my character. I remember that Rebbetzin Tzipora Heller, a noted lecturer, once recommended that we ask ourselves three questions when we are contemplating whether or not to do something:

(1) Can anyone else do this but me?

(2) Does this fit with my talents and gifts? (Can I really do this successfully?)

(3) Is this good for the individual or the community?

Should I watch my neighbor's child? Maybe her sister can do it. I'm good with children, but right now I have to think about how I feel, if I am physically up to it. If she needs help all of the time maybe it would be better for her and the child to find a more permanent solution. If this is a once-in-a-while request, then maybe it would be fine.

Should I agree to have this stranger over at my house for Shabbat? Maybe I have room, or maybe my house is too small and already full of people. Maybe my family loves having company or maybe they prefer peace and quiet. Maybe it is good for our community to encourage more people to come or maybe there are too many freeloaders.

Should I volunteer my services at my child's school? Maybe I have extra time or maybe I am already overextended. Maybe it is good for parents to help out or maybe the school should just hire someone else to do this particular job.

When I was overwhelmingly codependent, I didn't know that I could ask any questions. I felt that it was automatically my responsibility to say yes. As I got healthier, I came to realize that I must evaluate each situation. The outcome may look the same. I still took care of Harry and then Mom. The big difference is that by the time Mom came to live with us I had evaluated the situation and got appropriate help so that the entire burden would not fall on me. I was able to accept the time when we could no longer have her live at our house and looked for the best alternative possible.

I feel very blessed by my opportunity to take care of older people. I am grateful for the special times and the many lessons they have taught me about how to live life better. I am clearer about the purpose and meaning of my life. I pray that I will put the free time I have now to good use.

Sometimes I use these moments of time to reflect on all of the people who have come and gone in my life. Not only does death take people away, but some losses are the result of other circumstances. Children grow up. People get busy. Opportunities arise causing others to move away.

Then, as I reflect on all of these losses, a sense of panic begins to take over. Time is going so quickly — the hours, the days, the months and the years. I want to hold on to those seconds that are slipping away. Time passes and then it is gone. Gone are the people, the plans and the dreams. They seem to fly away.

Our brief physical existence is described in the Rosh Hashana *machzor* — the High Holiday prayer book. Just before the *Kedusha* section we are reminded that God does not want us to die but wants us to do *teshuva*, to return to him in repentance. We are told that God knows that we are just "flesh and blood," both originating and ending in "dust." The prayer continues to describe what we are like: "a broken shard, withering grass, a dissipating cloud, a blowing wind, flying dust and a fleeting dream."

King Solomon's words at the start of Ecclesiastes keep playing in my head like an endless tape. "*Hevel, havolim, hakol hevel*—Vanity of vanities, all is vanity." And what is the meaning of *hevel*? Emptiness, vanity, nothingness. Nothing in this physical life has any lasting value, any substance. It is all *hevel*, transient, soon to be gone and forgotten.

I suppose that my writing is an attempt to make something permanent, something that will last. But I know that this is also emptiness. The pages of my books will yellow with time, and the words will fade into oblivion.

I look at the beautiful pine tree outside my house, and I remember what a friend told me. "You know, pine trees don't last forever." How can that be? I just assumed that this giant pine tree would always be there. Yet, I am reminded that even this is not permanent.

Just as things get to be too much and I feel like I better stop reflecting or I will go crazy, I remember King Solomon's message: "In sum, after all has been heard, fear God and keep His commandments, for that is all of man" (Ecclesiastes, 12:13). Everything we know in this physical world is temporary. Only God is forever. My only chance to touch something of permanent value is by connecting myself to His will.

This is all I can do. I calm my racing mind and remind myself that all I can do is live in this moment and appreciate all that I have. I thank God for every precious moment and pray that I use each moment wisely. I know that I am a temporary being. The only true and enduring existence is God. I connect myself to Him, and in that way, I attach myself to eternity.

When I observe children building sandcastles at the beach, I realize that it is the process of building that is important—the laughter, the friendships, the development of skill and personality, the ability to work with others, the ability to work alone. To know that all the ebbs and tides of life will come and go, washing away our castles, and to choose to build anyway. To understand that the fun and excitement of life is in the activity of building.

What will you do? How will you live your life? What is the choice? Will you put enormous energy into material accomplishments or apply that energy to refine your character, improve relationships and build a connection to God? Will you choose the material or the spiritual, physical comfort or growth in wisdom and understanding? These are the choices that we make all of the time.

So whose life is more valuable? Is a child's life less valuable if his sandcastle has been washed away? Are we less valuable when our plans get washed away? Are we better if we accomplish our goals? Are we useless if we are old or sick and can't figure out why we're still here?

The Torah tells us that every life is valuable. We never know what impact we are making on our own souls and on the souls of others. All of us have our own tasks to complete. All of us have our own special blend of abilities and talents. Only God knows the purpose of existence and how all of the pieces fit together.

When I put life back into perspective, I can think of all of the people who passed through my life with a sense of appreciation. Each person added something to my life. My father was generous throughout the years to both family and friends, and he was diligent in making arrangements in the last year of his life to make sure that his resources would still help his children. He left me with gratitude for his gifts and an understanding of the importance of helping others.

Each Friday, when I bake my *challah* for Shabbat, I think of all the tips that Harry gave me. Harry used to make the best Miami onion rolls. One Friday I felt a little adventuresome. Armed with his instructions, I figured I could try. They weren't exactly like Harry's, but they were pretty good. It will probably take years before I come even close, but I'll keep trying. I will also keep the inspiration of Harry's kindness and concern for others along with his uncomplaining good nature.

From the residents at the Veterans home I hear

jokes and words of wisdom. They have also given me inspiration to face my challenges with courage and a positive attitude.

Each time that I go to a martial arts class, I am grateful to Mom. When I told her that I had enrolled my daughter Ilana, she had questioned me, "What about you? It is also important for you to learn how to defend yourself." She taught me that I also matter. Every time I look out my window, I think of her. She was right. We took down the bushes, and not only is it nicer outside but there is more light in the living room. When I go to the supermarket, I look for the carrots with the green grassy tops. I learned her lesson of looking for quality.

Most important, I have learned the importance of strength, the ability to stand firm and take care of myself when necessary. Mom took care of her family, helped her granddaughters and cooked hot soup for sick neighbors. She also knew how to be strong for herself, strong enough to last more than ninety years.

The sages teach us that we can learn from everyone around us. We have only to remain open to new possibilities and allow others to come into our lives. We can overcome our temporary existence when we let God into our lives. May we each find our own path to improve ourselves and the world as we connect ourselves to others, and to eternity, by attaching ourselves to the One who is true and enduring.

CHAPTER ELEVEN

HANGING
AROUND
OLD PEOPLE

Whenever I speak about taking care of older relatives in my home or working at the Veterans Home, I often get the same response. "How could you do that? It must be so depressing! I could never do that."

There is a lot of loss. Sometimes it is very sad, but the overall experience is not depressing. Working with old and dying people gives me a truer picture of what life is all about. It helps me to untangle my attachment to things that in the long run are really not so important. I see wives who center their lives around coming to visit their husbands in the Vets Home. I never hear them say that they were sorry that they didn't have a bigger house or a fancier car. Each wife holds her husband's hand and brags about the forty or fifty or more years of marriage. They talk about their lives together and about their children and grandchildren. They encourage their husbands to eat, walk or go outside for sunshine, and they make them smile and laugh. I understand that mundane matters such as dishes, laundry and bills must be taken care of, but their importance fades in comparison with the lives and relationships of loved ones. Living with a more accurate assessment of reality allows me to be more satisfied with my part in life, both the mundane and the spiritual. Ultimately, it has made me a happier person.

Rabbi Israel Lipschitz (1782-1860), author of the *Tiferet Yisroel*, a classic commentary on the Mishnah (the primary work of Jewish oral law), stated that since we live in a state "suspended between life and death," we are prescribed to view death, "our greatest enemy, with a tranquil heart." And so, being mindful of death will benefit both the body and the soul. Thoughts of death will help us to minimize our emphasis on physical needs and personal honor. It will also help us to increase our faith and trust in God and to still our fear of death. But the greatest benefit is to our souls because it will help to curb our evil inclination, pride and arrogance, which tend to lead us to sin. In the end, we all die, whether rich or poor, powerful or weak, educated or ignorant. Hope and courage will come from contemplating the eternal existence of our souls.

What is this soul that is often mentioned only briefly? I understand that, according to Judaism, our spiritual connection is not made by keeping our heads in the clouds. As my teacher Blema Feinstein told me, we can have our heads in the clouds from time to time, but our feet must be firmly planted on the ground. We make our connection with those worlds that we cannot see by following God's commandments in this world, the one we *can* see.

However, I need to know more. I need to know that there is a part of us that is eternal, that has a higher purpose, and that there is a reason to follow this often difficult path of doing God's will.

I've been told that the soul and life after our physical death is a difficult and complicated subject. I've been told that it is best not to focus too much on it. This may be true, but the great rabbis of the past weren't daunted by the task of explaining these concepts.

A PERSONAL REFLECTION

So I searched my heart to see how it feels about death.

Is it tranquil? Can I think about my own death without fear or worry? When I contemplate my inevitable death, how do I feel?

I am not sure that my heart is completely tranquil about this subject, but I know that I am not filled with fear. Death is everyone's ultimate reality, and I can calmly accept that. The pain that I do feel is the pain of loss, without the terror that accompanies the fear of death.

When I feel frightened of the possibility of facing sickness and old age, I remind myself that this is also part of God's plan. My best chance of coping with the knowledge of my own eventual decline, as well as the decline of the people I love, is to turn my will over to God and accept His plan for me and the world.

The soul is born against its will and will die against its will. I can understand this. I did not choose to be born, and I certainly will not choose to die. My birth and death are not in my control.

Only my moral choices are in my control. I can make good choices or bad ones. I can serve God's will or the desires of my very temporary physical body. The consequences of my choices will determine my place in eternity. In reality, much of the anguish my soul will feel upon death will be related to its inability to disconnect from my physical body.

According to *The Path of the Just*, humans were created for the sole purpose of rejoicing in God and deriving pleasure from the splendor of His Presence. It is written in *Ethics of the Fathers* that "One hour of the spiritual bliss in the World to Come is worth more than the whole life of this world." If you could gather all of the joys and pleasures from all of the people in this physical world, past and present, this still would not compare with a moment of spiritual pleasure of the World to Come.

A blissful spiritual existence in the presence of God does sound wonderful, but it is hard to really comprehend. I know that the sages regard death with regret, as the loss of opportunity to serve God and follow His commandments. I certainly appreciate how great a loss that is, but I will also feel sad to miss the many pleasures that God has given me in this physical part of my existence. The physical contact with another human being is something special and certainly something to be missed when it is gone. The warmth of a mother's hug and the big kisses from a loving grandfather. What could be sweeter than my baby falling to sleep gently in my arms or more reassuring than my husband's shoulder when I need to cry? At the same time, I console myself with the thought that there is an eternal place of goodness and reward. I only hope and pray that I will merit to be there. Being around old and dying people has forced me to come to terms with the losses we all experience in this physical life.

Taking care of Mom and all of the other older people in my life has changed me. I am not afraid to die, but I am also not afraid to live. My priorities are straighter than they were before and I relish each and every day. If my house is not perfectly clean and there is dirty laundry piled high, I try not worry. I could spend my entire existence on the mundane, constantly taking care of "business." But I won't do this. Other things are more important. Learning. Writing. Visiting Mom and Ezra. Talking to my daughter. Having lunch with my husband. Baking fresh *challah*. Walking in the morning. Resting in the sunshine.

It is true that I had to work on being able to take care of others without depleting myself. I want my giving to be real giving, not just my need to give. I want my giving to be in service of God, not in service of my own ego. Keeping that in mind, it turns out that taking care of Mom, as well as all of the other people in my life, has turned out to be taking care of myself.

I was sewing something quickly for my daughter that she wanted to wear one day. "Thank you Mommy!" she exclaimed.

"I only ask that you take care of my grandchildren as well as I take care of you!" I replied. Then I thought, "What did I mean by that statement?"

My parents were very giving. Most of my life they were giving and I was receiving. After about thirty years, I had the opportunity to be the giver. This was the greatest gift anyone could have bestowed upon me. I can only hope that my daughter will also have the opportunity to be a giver.

I am so grateful that I was given the opportunity to grow and learn as I cared for these three very special people—Daddy, Harry and Mom. What else can I say? Perhaps just—"Thank You."

CHAPTER TWELVE

TAKING CARE of MOM, TAKING CARE of ME

❧

"**E**verything is so hard for me," Mom said quietly. "Well, Mom, you are ninety-two," I reminded her.

It was the day before Rosh Hashana. I asked myself a question, "Do I clean for the holiday or go and visit Mom?" The house wasn't that messy. So, I opted for the visit.

I arrived around 11:00 a.m. Mom was already in the dining room waiting for lunch. She looked beautiful. She had on a new blouse and her hair was trimmed and combed very nicely. The thin, drawn look was gone. Her face was full and her skin was shining.

She wanted to walk, but it was very hard for her. I talked about Rosh Hashana and how I couldn't see her during the holiday since I could not walk there.

"It was easier when you lived with me," I said.

She nodded her head.

She ate almost all of her lunch and I tried to take her off the unit in a wheelchair. She stated very clearly, "Take me home!" (meaning her unit in the Hebrew Home.) She still managed to let us know what she wanted. She was more comfortable on the unit, and even though we may have felt more useful taking her for walks, this was where she wanted to be and she let us all know it in no uncertain terms. Valerie told me that Mom also got very angry with her when she did not take her back as soon as she made the request.

I was glad that she still displayed such strength. This was one of her many gifts that I was trying to receive.

I brought her back to her unit and took her into the lounge area where all of the residents gathered after lunch. She moved from the wheelchair into a big chair. Her anxiety dissipated. She relaxed. This was home.

Home had been so many places for Mom. As a small child, it was in a small shtetl in Poland. When her brothers moved to Warsaw to look for work, her father did not want to go. Her mother, Ida, said, "I'm taking my girls to Warsaw to be with my sons. You can come or not, it's up to you." He did go, and Warsaw became home. Then the boys moved to the United States to avoid being drafted into the Russian army. Life was very hard. Her father passed away. Mom told me that they would stand on line for hours for a few potatoes and a handful of rice. Her older sisters could not go out for fear that they would be attacked.

Finally, the boys sent money for them to come to America. Mom was twelve years old. Her temporary home became the ship at sea. When they arrived, Ida was sick. She had given her food to her children during the journey, and she became very malnourished. The people at Ellis Island wanted to send her back. They were afraid she had tuberculosis. The girls refused to leave their mother behind. They knew that she just needed food and rest. The boys brought food by rowboat each day. Finally, Ida got stronger and was able to go ashore. The Bronx became home.

Ida was an expert seamstress and worked to support her girls. When she became ill and could not work, Mom left school and took over her job. She was only fourteen. The other workers would hide her when the truant officer would come along. They needed the money.

I do not know any of the details of how my grandmother met my grandfather. I do know that Ida lived with them even after my father was born. The Bronx was still home. I do remember the walkup apartment building, which always smelled of homemade cooking as we ascended each flight of stairs. Of course the best smells were from my grandma's apartment—usually cabbage soup, both delicious and lethal!

I was only nine when my grandfather passed away. The Bronx would remain home for Mom for about another twenty years. Then, when it was too dangerous to walk the streets, Aunt Annette made arrangements for Mom to live in the Seniors' Apartment building on Columbus Avenue and 89th Street in Manhattan. I think she was there for about fifteen years when my home became her home for a very brief nine months. And now she was back in the Bronx. The dementia unit of the Hebrew Home for the Aged in Riverdale was now home.

I saw that her eyes were closing and she would soon be asleep.

"Let me kiss you good-bye before you fall asleep," I requested.

"You're leaving?" she asked.

"Yes," I replied, "but I'll be back soon."

ROSH HASHANA

Rosh Hashana was almost upon us. I began to think about what I regretted. I made my amends to Bob and Ilana. I had one more regret that I really could not resolve by myself. That regret was my past anxiety about time lost in "non-productive" activities. First when my father lived with us, then Harry and then Mom. I had many anxious moments, times when I worried about not being able to get things done, things like laundry, shopping and cleaning. I fretted that I did not have enough time to do the things I liked to do like walking, biking, learning or writing. I often felt overwhelmed, as if these frail people would live forever and I would be the eternal caretaker.

After Harry passed away, I still did not understand — I just did not get it. I could not explain this phenomenon in myself. I lived and worked with dying people all of the time, but death still shocked me. My mind may have known the truth, but my heart still lived with the illusion that life was forever.

My regret was for the needless anxiety, for my inability to realize that each of these loved ones would be with me for just a short time: my father for nine months, Harry for eight months and Mom for nine months. Why didn't I savor each moment as precious? Why did I ever feel moments of resentment or anxiety?

Of course, I knew the answer to my own questions. I was human. Perhaps my sense of eternity was a good thing. I just needed to remind myself that eternity did not exist in this physical world, but it did exist in God. We could not physically exist forever, but we could be a part of eternity if we connected with the Eternal One.

I finally connected with that paragraph in the Rosh Hashana service. Yes, we come from dust and our destiny is dust. We are like "withering grass" and "a passing shadow." But we are also God's children, and He loves us. We will make mistakes, but God will wait for us to return to him. As it says in the prayer book: "You do not wish the death of one deserving of death, but that he repent from his way and live." That promise is that life is eternal and that it will take place in the World to Come.

❧　　❧　　❧

As I clean up the bathroom after my teenage daughter, I make a mental note to remind her once again to pick up after herself. However, the anger is gone. I realize that time will fly by and one day, with God's help, she will be married and gone from my house. Even as I pick up yet another sock from the floor, I can now appreciate the preciousness of even this mundane moment. I also know that by helping me develop this additional perspective and gratitude, Daddy, Harry, and Mom have each helped me to inch a little closer in my connection to the Eternal.

MY PRAYER

I try to pray every day. Most of the time I use the formalized words that are written in my prayer book.

Personally asking for God's help is more difficult for me. I often struggle with the idea that it is okay to ask and I struggle to find the right words.

The struggle has paid off. I have learned that it is good for me to pray directly to God for help. Sometimes, I get to see the answer.

I have always felt very connected to Mom. I even look like her. So it felt natural for me to pray for her.

The first time that I tried was when she stopped eating. I prayed each day, "God, please watch over my Rivke bas Edal, please keep her eating." Within a week, she began to eat again.

The second time was a few months after she had broken her hip. After physical therapy had helped her to walk again, she insisted on walking unaided to the point of exhaustion. I was worried that she was going to fall again. So I added another request to my prayer. "God, please watch over my Rivke bas Edal, please keep her eating and keep her safe."

The next time I returned to the home I found her in the wheelchair. Her legs had locked and she could no longer stand. The nurses said that it was arthritis. This was not exactly what I anticipated or what I would have chosen, but she was safe.

The spring arrived. Passover came and left. I met Valerie at the Home.

"Oy, Oy."

Mom kept repeating this over and over as she kept trying to stand up from her wheelchair. She seemed so frustrated and unhappy at not being able to get up out of her chair.

I added a third request to my prayer. "Please God, please watch over my Rivke bas Edal, please keep her eating, please keep her safe, please help her to find and maintain a sense of peace."

My sister called me the next week after she visited with Mom.

She told me, "I'm really worried about Mom."

"Why, what's wrong?" I asked.

"I'm not sure, but for the first time I feel like she is going to die."

"Why would you say that?"

"I don't know, but she seemed different."

"How was she different?" I pressed on, anxiously.

"During the whole visit she seemed so peaceful."

On my next visit I also saw the change. She smiled and looked so happy to see me. Thank God, she was not dying at the moment. She was just calmer and more peaceful.

We are not always able to perceive the answer to our prayers. But with Mom, I was blessed in this way. I was able to experience God's mercy. Taking care of Mom has truly been taking care of me.

EPILOGUE

I was recently driving my daughter to an appointment. I was very tired and feeling a little sorry for myself. I thought, "I am always taking care of people. There's no one out there to take care of me!" Then I corrected my thought. "God is out there," I said to myself. "God is taking care of me." I felt a sense of peace. Yes, God has sent many special people into my life and I always get what I need for each crisis and in each period of turmoil.

I had intended on going to see Mom the next day. The weather report was for rain. I thought about going that morning instead but decided not to go because I was so tired. It is such an arduous trip. Besides, the weather reports are often incorrect. Maybe it would be a nice day.

I woke up to a cloudy sky. The weather report was ominous. Within an hour it started to rain. Then the rain turned to sleet.

I felt bad that I hadn't been able to go the day before. Between my schedule and the winter weather, I probably wouldn't be able to visit for another week. I thought of poor Mom, all alone in the nursing home.

Then I corrected my thought. She is not alone. God is there also. She will also get what she needs whether I am there or not. I felt more at peace.

Now I finally understand the line in Psalm 27, that even when our parents abandon us, God will not. He will always be there. We don't mean to abandon each other but we are human. There are limits to what we can accomplish. God has no limits. God is all good, all knowing and all powerful. Mom and I are both safe in His hands.

Then came the spring. The obstacles of bad weather were replaced by those of busy times. Since my husband is a C.P.A., I was always juggling a demanding tax season with the preparations for Pesach. After Pesach there was a bit more time.

At this point, Mom was dying. It was only a matter of when. I went to see her as often as I could. Sometimes she would open her eyes and just look at me. I sang her Yiddish songs and held her hand. I wanted to be there for her.

I went to a JACS convention upstate and stopped by the Home on the way up and on the way down. Mostly she was sleeping, but that afternoon on my way home she opened her eyes and looked at me for over an hour. I poured out my heart and told her all the things that I felt needed to be said — just in case...

Then a week went by before I was able to make another visit. I got a call on the day I was planning to go. It was May 16, the 23rd day of the month of *Iyar*. I was too late. She had died during the early morning hours. I met my sister and my niece Wendy at the home later that morning. We sat with Mom in her room until the funeral director arrived. We packed up her few things and planned her funeral. Once again, I was abandoned by a loved one.

There is so much death and so much loss in this temporary world. How do we continue on? I once read a beautiful article. Mr. Leibel Kuttner had lost his wife and eight children during the Holocaust. Everyone in his community had lost both family and friends. Someone asked him, "What will be with us?" He answered by first telling how King David's life as a shepherd was so pleasant and carefree. After being anointed as King, his troubles began. Someone else would have thrown away the crown and returned to his former stress-free life. David, of course, realized that his former life was not his but on loan from God and he completely accepted God's will and continued to praise Him in the midst of his troubles. Then Mr. Kuttner reminded his associate that the same was true of all that they had in the past. Wives, children, friends, an easy life — none are truly ours, just borrowed from God. The question you need to ask is "What will you do now with your present circumstances?"

My loved ones and good times were on loan. I am so grateful to God for all of the wonderful family and goodness that has been in my life. I feel comforted by the knowledge that Mom and I are still safely in His hands, along with everyone else. She is in a place that is more blissful than any we can imagine. I will try to figure out what it is that I am supposed to be working on now. May we all merit a place in the next world. May we all merit God's care and protection. May we all merit His peace.

SUGGESTED READING LIST

The Book of Knowledge by Maimonides

The Book of Ecclesiastes (*Kohelet*)

The Gates of Repentance by Rabbeinu Yona of Gerona

The Path of the Just by Rabbi Moshe Chaim Luzzato

Responsa of Rav Moshe Feinstein, Volume 1, Care of the Critically Ill, translated by Rabbi Moshe Dovid Tendler, KTAV Publishing House

Immortality, Resurrection, and the Age of the Universe: A Kabbalistic View, by Rabbi Aryeh Kaplan, KTAV Publishing House

The Jewish Way in Death and Mourning, by Rabbi Maurice Lamm, Jonathan David Publishers

Gesher Hachaim, The Bridge of Life: Life as a Bridge Between Past and Future, by Rabbi Tucazinsky, Moznaim Publishing Corp.

ABOUT THE AUTHOR

SIMA DEVORAH SCHLOSS works as a Recreational Therapist with geriatric residents at the Long Island State Veterans Home in Stony Brook, New York. She holds a B.A. in Music from Hartt College and an M.A. from Adelphi University. She lives in Stony Brook with her husband, Robert and her daughter, Ilana. She can be reached at SimaDevorah@aol.com and would love to hear your comments.